D0830308

THE TRUE JUSTICE OF A JUST GOD

THE TRUE JUSTICE OF A JUST GOD

Discovering God's Redemptive Plan for Mankind

LAWRENCE A. PANARELLO

iUniverse, Inc.
New York Lincoln Shanghai

The True Justice of a Just God
Discovering God's Redemptive Plan for Mankind

Copyright © 2007 by Lawrence A. Panarello

All rights reserved. No part of this book may be used or reproduced by any means, graphic, electronic, or mechanical, including photocopying, recording, taping or by any information storage retrieval system without the written permission of the publisher except in the case of brief quotations embodied in critical articles and reviews.

iUniverse books may be ordered through booksellers or by contacting:

iUniverse
2021 Pine Lake Road, Suite 100
Lincoln, NE 68512
www.iuniverse.com
1-800-Authors (1-800-288-4677)

ISBN: 978-0-595-41546-5 (pbk)
ISBN: 978-0-595-88183-3 (cloth)
ISBN: 978-0-595-85893-4 (ebk)

Printed in the United States of America

The views expressed in this work are solely those of the author and do not necessarily reflect the views of the publisher, and the publisher hereby disclaims any responsibility for them.

All Scriptures were cited from the Holy Bible, King James Version, unless otherwise noted.

Capitalization of Holy Spirit was used when referring to God as the Holy Spirit. Lower case of holy spirit was used when referring to God's gift of holy spirit.

Famous quotations were used by the author for the reader's enjoyment.

To Connie Panarello,
my wife and life partner, who inspires my heart

For I know him, that he will command his children and his household after him, and they shall keep the way of the Lord, to do justice and judgment; that the Lord may bring upon Abraham that which he hath spoken of him.

—Genesis 18:19

CONTENTS

ACKNOWLEDGMENTS

With grateful thanksgiving to God, I very much appreciate the love, prayers, and support of the believing ones of Beloved of God Ministries; you have helped me bring this message to print.

My personal and sincerest thanks to Greg and Alicia Hutt for their encouragement and labors of love to carry out the work set before us.

Love and thanks to Al and Marian Metzger, for their quotation contributions, editing assistance, and prayers for the success in fulfilling this endeavor.

Thanks to my daughter and son-in-law, David and Kristyne Crawley, whose encouragement has blessed my life beyond measure and to my grandsons, David and Michael, whose pure hearts will see great things.

Love to my dear and special aunt, Fil Livoti, who cannot wait to read my book.

Heartfelt gratitude goes to Stephen Contini, attorney and legal counsel, who at our first meeting inspired me to write this book.

My deep appreciation is due Jose and Wanda Gautier and their staff at Accurate Word, for printing the first draft of my manuscript.

My heart overflows with gratitude to my heavenly Father for every teacher and speaker of God's Word my ears have been blessed to hear that has enriched my heart with the knowledge of God and his wonderful Son.

And to you, the reader, I am respectfully appreciative for the joy of declaring unto you that God is light, and in him is no darkness at all.

INTRODUCTION

This then is the message which we have heard of him, and declare unto you, that God is light, and in him is no darkness at all. (1 John 1:5)

The illuminating truth "that God is light, and in him is no darkness at all," is a message that has not been fully realized by the Christian community-at-large. Born-again ones will quickly concur with this Scripture. Yet they contradict its veracity in both their speech and actions because of previous teaching or life experience that seems to attribute evil to God.

As enlightened as the Christian church has become over the centuries since the coming of Jesus Christ, many members of the family of God accept catastrophes, "natural" disasters, and calamities as "acts of God." Sayings such things as "All things happen for a purpose" or "God works in mysterious ways" harbor the implication that these maladies are somehow the work of God, and that he teaches us through tragedy. Is this what Christ came to declare? Is this the record of the first-century church? Are these the lessons we must learn in hopes of a future life with God? Is God really this stern ruler and wrathful judge?

I believe the Bible teaches that God is always good as clearly demonstrated in the life and ministry of Jesus Christ. When we understand the dynamics of the words employed in the Scriptures, the figures of speech understood among the people in biblical times, and the revealing of an evil spirit kingdom, we will take our first steps in walking with a gracious, loving Father who is light, and in whom there is no darkness at all.

The Greek word translated *message* in 1 John 1:5 means to decree a promise. It is "a technical term at law" meaning "the delivery of a judgment."[1] When the ministry of Jesus is considered in terms of a fully pre-

xvi The True Justice of a Just God

sented legal case with all of the testimony considered, all of the evidence thoroughly examined, and the verdict rendered, what did the believers who walked with God find as a result? That God is light, and in him is no darkness at all. What the church of the first century found should be experienced and proclaimed by believers today; they ought to "walk in the light, as he is in the light" (1 John 1:7).

Two of the great figures of speech employed in 1 John 1:5 eloquently emphasize and clarify that God is light. The first is *syncatabasis,* meaning "a going down together with."[2] That is, God submits with good grace to man's ignorance or inability to comprehend by taking on the attributes of inanimate things in order to convey a deeper truth: for example, *God is light.*

God is not literally "light;" he is incorporeal and invisible. This simple metaphor represents the essence and virtue of God in a way that mankind can understand: illumination, warmth, openness, purity, safety, life, goodness, goodwill, etc. are all attributes of God in his relationship towards mankind.

The second is *pleonasm,* meaning "more full."[3] This conveys an expression or phrase repeated in another form (many times in the opposite), to make its truth more explicit. In this verse, "God is light," is one phrase. It is then repeated in an opposing form, "in him is no darkness at all." The truth that God is light is contrasted against darkness, articulating that in him there is "no darkness at all."

"No … at all" in the Greek is a double negative, and so in this verse it accentuates the truth that in God there is not even the slightest hint of darkness or ill intent. God had John painstakingly preserve this emphatic truth so that the newly born-again ones would know the fullness of joy of walking with the Father.

During the times recorded in the Old Testament, believing ones had an awareness of God's goodness, love, compassion, mercy, and kindness; however, God was only able to reveal as much of himself and the spiritual realities surrounding them as they were capable of handling and receiving. The record of Moses, in Exodus 33, gives us some insight into this great truth of mankind's limited ability to grasp the magnitude of God.

> *And he [Moses] said, I beseech thee, shew me thy glory. And he [God] said, I will make all my goodness pass before thee, and I will proclaim the name of the Lord before thee; and will be gracious to whom I will be gracious, and will shew mercy on whom I will shew mercy. And it shall come to pass, while my glory passeth by, that I will put thee in a clift of the rock, and will cover thee with my hand while I pass by: And I will take away mine hand, and thou shalt see my back parts: but my face shall not be seen. (Exodus 33:18, 19, 22, 23)*

Moses could only see the "back parts" or the after effects of God. At this point, he did not comprehend God completely and openly—to behold the "face" of God. As Moses grew, God was able to reveal to Moses some of the purposes behind his ways, while the children of Israel only saw God's mighty acts. As recorded, "He [God] made known his ways unto Moses, his acts unto the children of Israel" (Psalms 103:7).

Therefore, when it came to the ability to recognize an antithetical, negative, spiritual kingdom at work in the world, the Old Testament believers were even more limited. God could not reveal to mankind the depth and extent of this evil kingdom's influence and power in the events of this world because of the weaknesses of the flesh and the terror such knowledge would inspire. Under the Old Testament and the law before the coming of Christ, mankind was not equipped to deal with this evil domain.

Consequently, God took upon himself the burden of responsibility for all things, positive as well as negative, in order to in some way communicate with mankind. Thus, in the writing of the Bible, particularly the Old Testament, many Scriptures contain the Hebrew *idiom of permission*. In his research book *Figures Of Speech Used in the Bible* (1968), E. W. Bullinger explains that "active verbs [were] used by the Hebrews to express not the doing of the thing but the *permission* of the thing which the agent is said to do."[4] Hence God is not the perpetrator of evil, nor does he give his "permission" for evil to be done. God allowed for these acts of darkness to be attributed to him until the coming of Christ when the evil spirit realm would be openly revealed.

These Hebraic idioms of permission are found in such areas as Moses' apparent complaint to God in Exodus after he and Aaron confronted Pharaoh to let the children of Israel hold a feast to God in the wilderness. In response, Pharaoh ordered the taskmasters to withhold straw from the Hebrews for making bricks, without allowing the tally to decrease.

> *And Moses returned unto the Lord, and said, Lord, wherefore hast thou so evil entreated this people? Why is it that thou hast sent me? For since I came to Pharaoh to speak in thy name, he hath done evil to this people; neither hast thou delivered thy people at all. (Exodus 5:22–23)*

Moses understood that it was not God who mistreated the people with evil. Pharaoh, under the influence of Satan, caused the people to serve in bitter bondage. Satan was no friend to the Egyptians, either. Before each successive plague that came into Egypt, Moses forewarned Pharaoh and extended God's merciful hand of deliverance to this oppressor if he would let God's people go. Through hardness of heart, Pharaoh rejected God's offers of salvation. Satan, exercising his legal authority over his dominion, wreaked havoc upon the land of Egypt and its people.

Another record where this idiom is employed is in regard to Uzzah, the son of Abinadab of the tribe of Judah, in whose house the Ark of the Covenant was placed when it was returned by the Philistines. Uzzah tragically died when he touched the ark to steady it when the cattle transporting it stumbled.

> *And when they came to Nachon's threshing floor, Uzzah put forth his hand to the ark of God, and took hold of it; for the oxen shook it. And the anger of the Lord was kindled against Uzzah; and God smote*

him there for his *error; and there he died by the ark of God. (2 Samuel 6:6–7)*

The Kohathites bore the responsibility of transporting the holy things of the tabernacle, including the ark of God (Numbers 4). All Israelites were warned that touching the holy things would result in death. Uzzah (not a Kohathite), being well aware of this safety admonition from God, made a fatal mistake by touching the ark. Uzzah's death was no more caused by God than the electrocution of a man touching a clearly marked power line would be the fault of the electric company. Are these events tragic? Definitely! However, God gave clear warnings and instructions to avoid the danger. Again, by permission, God accepts that the people attribute to him the ensuing consequence.

The American Heritage Dictionary, Second Edition (1991), defines *idiom* as "a speech form or expression of a given language that is peculiar to itself grammatically or that cannot be understood from the individual meaning of the elements."[5] The saying expressed may be exactly the opposite of the words employed or even unrelated to the wordage. Yet the actual meanings of such phrases are generally understood by the common people. There are many clear examples in our current English vernacular such as:

- "Easy come, easy go." The inference is not that there is very little effort expended to obtain something. It is often just the opposite. The meaning conveyed is that you are not going to fret about its loss. You had it, it's gone, you move on.

- "Come rain or come shine." Here the meaning has nothing to do with the weather, but rather, is an expression of your determination to accomplish something.

In Job 1:21, Job's comment "the Lord gave, and the Lord hath taken away; blessed be the name of the Lord," means if things go well, praise the

Lord! If they do not go well, you still praise the Lord because you know your deliverance will come from the Lord.

There is a divine purpose for the usage of the *idiom of permission* in the Bible. Not only were the believers unequipped to effectively handle the evil spirit realm; this idiom placed God at the forefront of people's thoughts and speech. It served to prevent the evil spirits from receiving infamous notoriety and attention from the people of God. God exhorted Israel on this point in Exodus 23:13: "And in all *things* that I have said unto you be circumspect [to hedge and protect]: and make no mention of the name of other gods, neither let it be heard out of thy mouth."

Misunderstanding legitimate, grammatical expressions used in the Old Testament and failing to grasp the limited ability of mankind to understand the spirit realm before the coming of Jesus Christ have confused many Christian communities of today. This confusion has inadvertently hampered many believing ones from walking in the dynamics and fearlessness originally experienced, as recorded throughout the book of Acts.

The ministry of Jesus Christ was, in essence, man's first real foray into the existence of an evil spirit realm and an exposition as to how it functioned. Jesus uncovered this sinister domain and its manipulation over lives and earthly events. As recorded in Ephesians 6:12, "For we wrestle not against flesh and blood, but against principalities, against powers, against the rulers of the darkness of this world, against spiritual wickedness in high *places*." Again in Colossians 2:15, "*And* having spoiled principalities and powers, he made a shew of them openly, triumphing over them in it." Prior to Christ, mankind's perspective of the origin of evil was in reference mainly to peoples, nations, and tribes.

Jesus, at the same time, was revealing the purity of God: his perfect love, his tender mercies, his grace, his compassion, and his good will toward mankind. In all the revelation of Jesus Christ's life, ministry, and testimony, he demonstrated that God was good always, and that in God was indeed no darkness at all. As John later wrote, "No man hath seen

God at any time; the only begotten Son, which is in the bosom of the Father, he hath declared *him*" (John 1:18). Who would have a more intimate relationship with God than he who "is in the bosom of the Father"?

According to the *Theological Dictionary of the New Testament* (Kittel, 1933), *declare* means "to be the introducer." It is "a technical term for the exposition of poets," or "of laws."[6] For example, in the United States, the legislative branch writes the laws. The judicial branch interprets the written laws. They are supposed to provide the understanding and proper application of these laws in harmony with the Constitution, according to the intent of the founding fathers. Similarly, Jesus Christ introduced the heart of the Father. His life provided an exposition for the understanding and proper application of the Scriptures in harmony with the nature of God and according to the purpose of the heavenly Father.

In Greek religious terminology, *declare* infers a revealing, or a taking away the shroud from under the veil; simply put, it is to do away with the mystique. Jesus came to introduce God to mankind, to take away the veil and the mystique regarding him, showing his true heart and good intent in his relationship with mankind. Jesus showed and declared that God is light.

In this declaration of God, there is not one record of Jesus Christ ever injuring anyone, causing pain to anyone, making anyone sick, or causing anyone to die. His purpose and ministry was to clearly and fully declare or introduce the Father, as seen in these three excerpts:

> *Then said Jesus unto them, When ye have lifted up the Son of man, then shall ye know that I am he, and that I do nothing of myself; but as my Father hath taught me, I speak these things. And he that sent me is with me: the Father hath not left me alone; for I do always those things that please him. (John 8:28–29)*
>
> *I and my Father are one. (John 10:30)*

Jesus saith unto him, Have I been so long time with you, and yet hast thou not known me, Philip? he that hath seen me hath seen the Father; and how sayest thou then, Shew us the Father? (John 14:9)

If we have seen Jesus Christ, as revealed in the Gospels, through both his words and his works, we have truly seen the Father. Jesus revealed that God was not a stern ruler and wrathful judge, but rather a deliverer and a healer. People may declare that God gave them a sickness or an infirmity to keep them humble; however, that is not what Jesus declared of God. There is no such incident recorded in the life and ministry of our Lord to support that inference. As a matter of truth, every action in his life and ministry contradicted and refuted that kind of allegation. Bear in mind the admonition in Isaiah 5:20, "Woe unto them that call evil good, and good evil; that put darkness for light, and light for darkness; that put bitter for sweet, and sweet for bitter!" It is the misunderstanding of the full purpose of Christ's ministry that has kept God under the veil and shroud of the Old Testament. Unacquainted with the idioms employed, men and women attribute to God actions which he has not done.

When we hear of the sudden death of someone who loved God, it is sometimes said, "God called him home." We see his grieving widow, his children left fatherless and without his care. Perhaps in the secret thoughts of our hearts, we ponder how God could need that someone more than his grieving widow or his fatherless children? Yet we try to be positive and say, "God took him," because we are afraid to admit we do not understand and do not want to accuse God of evil. So we call it one of "the mysteries of God," or we say, "God works in mysterious ways" or "You must have faith." All the while, no matter how you sugarcoat it, death is darkness and death is evil.

The Scriptures document the devil has the power of death. Hebrews 2:14 declares, "Forasmuch then as the children are partakers of flesh and blood, he [Jesus Christ] also himself likewise took part of the same; that through death he might destroy him that had the power of death, that is, the devil." The fact that this beloved one died in no way indicates fault or evil on his part any more than the death of a soldier indicates defect or disloyalty. Death is an enemy! Concerning this enemy, 1 Corinthians 15:26 assures us, "The last enemy *that* shall be destroyed *is* death." Death steals from the world a life, a child, a parent, a spouse, a witness to the light and mercy of God. If death were to bring us into the glory and presence of God, it would not be an enemy but rather, our hope.

Sickness and death are darkness. Jesus Christ came to deliver mankind from both, and ultimately, we will get to enjoy the victory over both for all eternity. But if sickness, death, and darkness are a part of God now, we have no hope. Darkness would pursue us beyond the gathering together (commonly referred to as the Rapture), and the Resurrections, because the Bible asserts God does not change (Malachi 3:6), and Jesus Christ remains the same (Hebrews 13:8). Thankfully, sickness and death are *not* a part of the true God or his wonderful Son. Our hope is the return of Christ, with the overthrow of death, bringing us into the glory and presence of God. In God is life—not death. John 1:4 says, "In him was life; and the life was the light of men."

Life is energy that imparts animation and vitality, a means of self power. The birth place for all life is in God! He is the author of life, and through life he illuminates the way for mankind. "In him was life; and the life was the light of men" (I John 1:4).

God is light, and he is also love. He never contemplates evil; for love "thinketh no evil" (1 Corinthians 13:5). It is not a consideration. God does not need darkness to accomplish good. If that were true, when evil or darkness ends, so must good. But God is light, in all of its glory and perfection. In that beauty and perfection is eternity to enjoy his goodness unabated.

To attain to true justice requires that the one judging be not flawed. The true God, the Father of our Lord Jesus Christ, is perfect; and thus, the spiritual laws of life he has set in motion are also perfect. The basic premise for writing *The True Justice of a Just God* is the underlying truth that God is light and that in him, there is no darkness.

As the perfect judge, full of compassion and mercies, having absolute understanding of the operations of the evil spirit realm, as well as the weaknesses of the flesh, God has chosen to look upon the heart (1 Samuel 16:7). May our hearts rest assured by the Psalm of David, "Like as a father pitieth *his* children, *so* the Lord pitieth them that fear him. For he knoweth our frame; he remembereth that we *are* dust" (Psalms 103:13–14). His will is salvation for all (1 Timothy 2:4).

The book of Revelation tells us that a new heaven and a new earth are coming. In them there will be no more death, there will be no more pain, and there shall be no more night because the Lord God will give them light. Why? The truth is—God is light. There are many things we do not know about life and about God. One thing we do know, or can know because of Jesus Christ, is that in him there is no darkness at all!

CHAPTER I:
THE TRUE JUSTICE OF A JUST GOD

◆　　◆　　◆

We are all full of weakness and errors; let us mutually pardon each other our follies. It is the first law of nature.

—Voltaire

◆　　◆　　◆

It is innate in mankind to want some form of justice. Whether it is solely for the individual or for the society as a whole, mankind has a desire to have a wrong righted, an offense recompensed. Whether in a criminal or civil case, justice is generally equated with revenge; that is, with the injured party being sufficiently satisfied by the punishment administered to the offender.

Societies have looked to rules and rulers to provide a system by which nations, tribes, or peoples may symbiotically be enjoined. From the singular despot or shaman, who may rule by whim or superstition, to elected bodies, these forms of governance are ordained by men to define ways to recompense the injured through the punishment of wrongdoers.

This book will not particularly address criminal matters. This is rather a consideration of forms of judicial review available to the Judean people during the biblical times and the ultimate true justice of a just God.

Three forums for settling disputes or claims were available in the early culture of the Bible lands. People could seek redress through the following

1

recognized bodies for the administration of justice: a form of civil court or tribunal, the elders of the gate, and the daysman.[1]

CHAPTER II:
THE CIVIL COURT OR
TRIBUNAL

The children of Israel always had access to an institution for civil complaints. Even when they were in servitude to another nation or people, a justice system existed for the protection of the general populous. While under occupation and when the Israelites were dispersed among many nations, they were often allowed a certain amount of autonomous rule and a process of self-adjudication. Perhaps the founding of a tribunal or civil court for the children of Israel may be implied when Moses was commanded by God to ordain the seventy elders.

> *And the Lord said unto Moses, Gather unto me seventy men of the elders of Israel, whom thou knowest to be elders of the people, and officers over them; and bring them unto the tabernacle of the congregation, that they may stand there with thee. And I will come down and talk with thee there: and I will take of the spirit which is upon thee, and will put it upon them; and they shall bear the burden of the people with thee, that thou bear it not thyself alone. (Numbers 11:16–17)*

The same spirit (the connection by which God, who is Spirit, could communicate with man, who is flesh) that was upon Moses was the necessary ingredient to equip these elders of the people to accomplish the work for which they were chosen. In fact, Moses adds in verse 29, "would God that all the Lord's people were prophets, *and* that the Lord would put his spirit upon them!"

From the set of seventy elders, Jewish tradition traces the origins to its Sanhedrin council, which functioned as Israel's Supreme Court. *The Catholic Encyclopedia, Volume XIII, OnlineEdition,* (2003) states:

> *An institution as renowned as the Sanhedrin was naturally given by Jewish tradition a most venerable and hollowed antiquity. Some Doctors, indeed, did not hesitate to recognize the Sanhedrin in the Council of the seventy Elders founded by Moses (Numbers 11:16); others pretended to discover the first traces of the Sanhedrin in the tribunal created by Josaphat [Jehoshaphat] (2 Chronicles 19:8): but neither of these institutions bears, in its composition or in its attributions, any resemblance to the Sanhedrin as we know it. Nor should the origin of the Sanhedrin be sought in the Great Synagogue, of which tradition attributed the foundation to Esdras [Ezra]; and which it considered as the connecting link between the last of the Prophets and the first Scribes: for aside from the obscurity hovering over the functions of this once much-famed body, its very existence is, among modern scholars, the subject of the most serious doubts. Yet it may be that from the council of the nobles and chiefs and ancients, on which the ruling of the restored community devolved at the time of Nehemias [Nehemiah] and Esdras [Ezra] (Nehemiah 2:16; 4:8, 13; 5:7; 7:5; Ezra 5:5, 9; 6:7, 14; 10:8), gradually developed and organized, sprang up the Sanhedrin. At any rate, the first undisputed mention we possess touching the* gerousia *of Jerusalem is connected with the reign of Antiochus the Great (223–187* B.C.*; Joseph. "Antiq.", XII, iii, 3).* [1]

The Sanhedrin consisted of seventy-one members, which included the president of the council. This makeup likely reflected Moses plus the seventy elders. Candidates selected to be part of this notable body would be well schooled in the oral traditions, Talmudic writings, and the Torah. Aspirants would no doubt have sat under the tutelage of a highly respected training center such as the rabbinical schools of Schammai and Hillel (where Gamaliel, spoken of in the book of Acts, taught).

> *Then stood there up one in the council, a Pharisee, named Gamaliel, a doctor of the law, had in reputation among all the people, and commanded to put the apostles forth a little space. (Acts 5:34)*

The argument has been made by some scholars that Paul either aspired to or was indeed a member of this assembly. Whichever, he was a rising star among the "best and brightest" and touted an impressive pedigree, as described in the following passages:

> *I am verily a man which am a Jew, born in Tarsus, a city in Cilicia, yet brought up in this city at the feet of Gamaliel, and taught according to the perfect manner of the law of the fathers, and was zealous toward God, as ye all are this day. (Acts 22:3)*

> *Circumcised the eighth day, of the stock of Israel, of the tribe of Benjamin, an Hebrew of the Hebrews; as touching the law, a Pharisee. (Philippians 3:5)*

> *For ye have heard of my conversation in time past in the Jews' religion, how that beyond measure I persecuted the church of God, and wasted it: And profited in the Jews' religion above many my equals in mine own nation, being more exceedingly zealous of the traditions of my fathers. (Galatians 1:13–14)*

Moses recognized the great necessity for the spirit of God, which God placed upon the seventy in order to share Moses' burden of hearing the disputes between the people. With the passing of time, the reliance on the spirit of God for judging gave way to intellectual and legal debate. As Matthew 23:23 points out, "the weightier *matters* of the law, judgment, mercy, and faith" became neglected. Without acting upon the spiritual connection point with God, who looks upon the heart, the responsibility for civil justice was not leavened with compassion, mercy, and forgiveness.

Neither would the people of God receive clemency from the powers of the foreign tribunals and judges. Hence, Jesus' exhortation:

> *Agree with thine adversary quickly, whiles thou art in the way with him; lest at any time the adversary deliver thee to the judge, and the judge deliver thee to the officer, and thou be cast into prison. Verily I say unto thee, Thou shalt by no means come out thence, till thou hast paid the uttermost farthing. (Matthew 5:25–26)*

These verses refer to going before the civil court. Many times the disagreeing parties would caravan to another city or locale to appear before the magistrate for judgment. The two parties would travel together with their lawyers, witnesses, and anyone else pertinent to the case. During the trip, they would have ample opportunity to talk and come to a conclusion before the proceedings ever occurred.[2]

Once actual litigation was initiated, the outcome strictly followed the prescribed statutes. If the accused was found guilty, punishment could be rather brutal; if it was determined the accused was innocent, the one bringing charges before the court could be severely fined or even imprisoned for making an accusation judged to be untrue. Cases rarely ended without punishment decreed to at least one party. Therefore, it was a wise decision for the parties to make amends and privately settle their dispute before it reached the courts.

Civil cases were a matter of public record. In a culture where lineage was a keystone of society, a negative judgment could impinge on a whole family's good name for years. Thus, the innocent often paid as dear a price as those deemed guilty.

◆   ◆   ◆

The sad duty of politics is to establish justice in a sinful world.
—Reinhold Neibuhr

◆   ◆   ◆

True justice in the Federal or Civil Court is an impossible task. In a world of spiritual realities, politics has chosen to handcuff itself to the carnal and suppress the recognition of God or spiritual matters. As such, politics can condemn but not convert and convict but not redeem.

The apostle Paul rebuked the believers in Corinth for allowing matters pertaining to the family of God to be brought to the civil courts and be open to criticism among those without spiritual understanding. He was well aware that true justice could not be served in the forum of the unbelieving; rather, only the defamation of God and the family of God could occur there. Paul wrote:

> *Dare any of you, having a matter against another, go to law before the unjust, and not before the saints? I speak to your shame. Is it so, that there is not a wise man among you? no, not one that shall be able to judge between his brethren? But brother goeth to law with brother, and that before the unbelievers. Now therefore there is utterly a fault among you, because ye go to law one with another. Why do ye not rather take wrong? why do ye not rather suffer yourselves to be defrauded? Nay, ye do wrong, and defraud, and that your brethren.* (1 Corinthians 6:1, 5–8)

Satan had really incited the members of the family of God at Corinth to injure one another. Rather than putting "ointment" upon the hurt, the born-again ones took their case before the unbelieving for judgment. As described in Jeremiah 8:22, "*Is there* no balm in Gilead; *is there* no physician there? why then is not the health of the daughter of my people recovered?"

The answer is simple. There was clearly a disregard for spiritual heart. and it is evident that some in the church at Corinth were not really interested in healing the wounds among the born-again ones, but rather were interested in serving their personal interests and/or recompensing their own injuries. In their hardness of heart and wrath, blinded by the temporal sting of the offence, they ignored Jesus' exhortation. They wanted others to suffer the pain they felt even more than they desired to be made whole.

◆   ◆   ◆

When will our consciences grow so tender that we will act to prevent human misery rather than avenge it?

—Eleanor Roosevelt

◆   ◆   ◆

Influenced by unbelief, divisions began to arise, first in their practice and then in their core beliefs. Ultimately, Satan saw to it that God and his Word were traduced and the veracity of the Scriptures was impugned. Jesus says of such situations:

> *For this people's heart is waxed gross, and* their ears *are dull of hearing, and their eyes they have closed; lest at any time they shall see with* their *eyes, and hear with* their *ears, and should understand with* their *heart, and should be converted, and I should heal them. (Matthew 13:15)*

In many situations, according to the law of the land, one person may be shackled in the prison house; while according to the laws of life, another may bear the shackles of an open wound inflicted by the offense. Only true justice, such as described in the following passage, can bring forth repentance as well as healing.

> *Recompense to no man evil for evil. Provide things honest in the sight of all men. If it be possible, as much as lieth in you, live peaceable with all men. Dearly beloved, avenge not yourselves, but* rather *give place unto wrath: for it is written, Vengeance* is *mine; I will repay, saith the Lord. Therefore if thine enemy hunger, feed him; if he thirst, give him drink: for in so doing thou shalt heap coals of fire on his head. Be not overcome of evil, but overcome evil with good. (Romans 12:17–21)*

In the biblical culture, a fire was kept burning in the village throughout the night for warmth, protection, and light. Just before the first light of the morning, the person tending the fire would take a piece of a broken water pitcher and place within the potsherd glowing coals. Carrying this potsherd on his head, he would be warmed through the insulation of the thick clay. As he delivered these glowing embers to his neighbors for the ignition of their morning fires for heating and cooking, they would be "warmed and fed." "Heap coals of fire on his head" is an eastern expression of good will, meaning that one's warmth and love may melt the heart of an enemy.[3]

There is an astonishing example and lesson in 2 Kings, of a great act of kindness and love to an enemy. This stunning record of a man, walking by the spirit of God and the revelation he received, stands as a monument of truth to God's goodness even in the midst of a war against his people, Israel.

> *Then the king of Syria warred against Israel, and took counsel with his servants, saying, In such and such a place shall be my camp. And the man of God [Elisha] sent unto the king of Israel, saying, Beware that thou pass not such a place; for thither the Syrians are come down. And the king of Israel sent to the place which the man of God told him and warned him of, and saved himself there, not once nor twice. (2 Kings 6:8–10)*

The king of Syria sought advice from his top generals on a strategic war plan to defeat Israel. With their counsel, he sent his army to places where they could ambush the army of Israel. But God, told Elisha [by revelation] the exact locations. Elisha, in turn, informed the king of Israel and saved the army on several occasions. In fact, this occurred so many times that the king of Syria suspected that his top-secret meetings had been infiltrated by a double agent.

Therefore the heart of the king of Syria was sore troubled for this thing; and he called his servants, and said unto them, Will ye not shew me which of us is for the king of Israel? And one of his servants said, None, my lord, O king: but Elisha, the prophet that is in Israel, telleth the king of Israel the words that thou speakest in thy bedchamber. And he said, Go and spy where he is, that I may send and fetch him. And it was told him, saying, Behold he is in Dothan. Therefore sent he thither horses, and chariots, and a great host: and they came by night, and compassed the city about. (2 Kings 6:11–14)

The king of Syria set up his own covert operation to find out Elisha's position. The king dispatched a huge contingent of special forces in a nighttime raid to encircle the city of Dothan where Elisha was staying. As they awaited orders to take Elisha captive, morning came.

And when the servant of the man of God was risen early, and gone forth, behold, an host compassed the city both with horses and chariots. And his servant said unto him, Alas, my master! how shall we do? And he [Elisha] answered, Fear not: for they that be with us are more than they that be with them. And Elisha prayed, and said, Lord, I pray thee, open his eyes, that he may see. And the Lord opened the eyes of the young man; and he saw: and, behold, the mountain was full of horses and chariots of fire round about Elisha. And when they came down to him, Elisha prayed unto the Lord, and said, Smite this people, I pray thee, with blindness. And he smote them with blindness according to the word of Elisha. (2 Kings 6:15–18)

Here we have the Hebrew *idiom of permission*, God allowing something to be attributed to him, although it is not through his action.[4] God is in the business of opening the eyes of the blind, physically as well as spiritually. Satan caused this malady. In the midst of this attack, God was able to protect Elisha, the servant, and the people of Dothan. God let Elisha know by revelation what Satan was planning; thus, Elisha prayed that God's grace and mercy be not extended to the Syrian army at this point. Reminiscent of Exodus 33:19, where God said, "[I] will be gracious to whom I will be gracious, and will shew mercy on whom I will shew mercy." The Syrian army would have destroyed a small city like Dothan. In their blind state, Elisha took advantage to lead them to Samaria, the capital, where the king of Israel and the armies of Israel were stationed.

> *And Elisha said unto them, This is not the way, neither is this the city: follow me, and I will bring you to the man whom ye seek. But he led them to Samaria. And it came to pass, when they were come into Samaria, that Elisha said, Lord, open the eyes of these men, that they may see. (2 Kings 6:19–20a)*

Now with this expeditionary force surrounded, Elisha entreats God's mercy and grace to open their eyes.

> *And the Lord opened their eyes, and they saw; and, behold, they were in the midst of Samaria. And the king of Israel said unto Elisha, when he saw them, My father, shall I smite them? shall I smite them? And he answered, Thou shalt not smite them: wouldest thou smite those whom thou hast taken captive with thy sword and with thy bow? set bread and water before them, that they may eat and drink, and go to their master. And he prepared great provision for them: and when they had eaten and drunk, he sent them away, and they went to their master. So the bands of Syria came no more into the land of Israel. (2 Kings 6:20b–23)*

As a result of this one magnificent act of kindness and a man walking by the spirit of God, Israel enjoyed more than forty years of peace with Syria. What an inspiring record of truth applied in overcoming evil with good.

♦   ♦   ♦

We ought always to deal justly, not only with those who are just to us, but likewise to those who endeavor to injure us; and this, for fear lest by rendering them evil for evil, we should fall into the same vice.

—Hierocles

♦   ♦   ♦

It is important to note God says that evil can be overcome by good. Light will always dispel darkness. The rate and extent to which it is dispelled is determined by the power of the luminary and the area to be lit. A candle in a darkened stadium may benefit only a small area; yet, the origin of the glow from the burning wick may be seen from any point.

Darkness gives no glory to the flame. Light is its own eminence. Neither the gloom of darkness nor the deep voids of space can quench the stars or halt their radiance. Neither time nor distance can interrupt light's majesty. People may close their eyes and deny light's attraction. Nevertheless, the light cannot be overcome, "And the light shineth in darkness; and the darkness comprehended it not [could not overcome it]" (John 1:5). Jesus told his disciples, "Let your light so shine before men, that they may see your good works, and glorify your Father which is in heaven" (Matthew 5:16).

Despite man's rejection and many offenses against God, Jesus Christ was not sent to impute our trespasses, but to reconcile us to God. Satan condemns man, but it is God who justifies man through belief in Christ.

For all have sinned, and come short of the glory of God; Being justified freely by his grace through the redemption that is in Christ Jesus: Whom God hath set forth to be a propitiation [full payment in the place of and on behalf of another] through faith in his blood, to declare his righteousness for the remission of sins that are past, through the forbearance of God; To declare, I say, at this time his righteous-

ness: that he [God] might be just, and the justifier of him which believeth in Jesus. (Romans 3:23–26)

Certainly, God could have had a "case" against mankind, but by love he chose to entreat him. Among the family of God, we are to follow this example and entreat and inspire one another to live lives of love in accordance with the Scriptures.

Let all bitterness, and wrath, and anger, and clamour, and evil speaking, be put away from you, with all malice: And be ye kind one to another, tenderhearted, forgiving one another, even as God for Christ's sake hath forgiven you. (Ephesians 4:31–32)

Forgiveness has a twofold release. It releases the offender from the condemnation of the trespass, and it releases the injured party from the burdens of bitterness and anger that arise from unresolved conflict. The harmful negative effects of resentment, despondence, and other emotions fester to degrade such mental strongholds as confidence and trust.

Soundness and wholeness cannot be sustained without forgiveness. As surely as microscopic bacteria deteriorates the flesh through an open wound and the physical systems of a body become compromised; lack of forgiveness allows Satan to undermine the moral fiber of the body of Christ and deprive it of the strength to stand against the unseen forces that seek its demise.

The standard for forgiveness is set. We, who were once dead in trespasses and sin against God, were forgiven. When we were enemies of God, his goodness melted the coldness and hardness of our hearts. As born-again ones, shouldn't we now be able to forgive one another?

◆   ◆   ◆

He who cannot forgive others breaks the bridge over which he must pass himself, for every man needs to be forgiven.

—Lord Herbert

◆   ◆   ◆

CHAPTER III:
THE ELDERS OF THE GATE

Another forum where a case could be presented was before the "elders of the gate" or elders of the city.[1] This body was selected from among the people to administer justice in accordance with religious ordinance, custom, and culture. This was a more localized justice system.

The elders generally sat at the main gate of the city to dispense this sacred service to the people of God; hence, their title. Public notices and legal decisions were fastened to the gate for the community, visitors, and merchants to read as they came into the city to shop at the markets or do other commerce. For instance, if someone defaulted in business, a list detailing the indebtedness and creditors would be posted by the elders of the gate at the entrance to the city so passing merchants could be aware of the bankrupt individual's situation and avoid doing business with the indebted one.

However, were the insolvency resolved, the business owner would be given a fresh start. Upon clearing the indebtedness, the elders of the gate would fold the notice, covering the former debts, and post it back on the door, indicating all had been repaid. The past debt would be sealed from sight.[2] This can be seen as an illustration of Christ's work on the cross.

And you [Even you], being dead in your sins and the uncircumcision of your flesh, hath he quickened [made alive] together with him, having forgiven you all trespasses; Blotting out the handwriting of ordinances that was against us, which was contrary to us, and took it out of the way, nailing it to his cross. (Colossians 2:13–14)

Jesus Christ was our redeemer, fully paying for our sins and covering us in God's righteousness. A verse in Isaiah becomes very clear when we understand this magnificent truth.

> *Speak ye comfortably to [the heart of] Jerusalem, and cry unto her, that her warfare [hardship] is accomplished, that her iniquity is pardoned: for she hath received of the Lord's hand double for all her sins. (Isaiah 40:2)*

The inhabitants of Jerusalem were pardoned. Receiving "of the Lord's hand double" means the notice was folded over, covering all their sins. They were cleared of their indebtedness for sin.[3]

The elders of the gate were to be well trained in the Scriptures and traditions, and at the same time, readily demonstrate great heart toward the family of God. God honored their commissioning and dedication to this sacred service. He equipped them to meet the needs of his people by placing his spirit upon them.

They were responsible to handle the most personal and private situations. These incidents and situations were to be judged in accordance with the heart and desire of God for healing and deliverance. For example:

> *If any man take a wife, and go in unto her, and hate her, And give occasions of speech against her, and bring up an evil name upon her, and say, I took this woman, and when I came to her, I found her not a maid: Then shall the father of the damsel, and her mother, take and bring forth the tokens of the damsel's virginity unto the elders of the city in the gate: And the damsel's father shall say unto the elders, I gave my daughter unto this man to wife, and he hateth her. (Deuteronomy 22:13–16)*

Clearly, they were involved in very intimate and complicated circumstances. If the charge was true, harsh consequences could result for the woman.

But if this thing be true and the tokens of virginity be not found for the damsel: Then they shall bring out the damsel to the door of her father's house, and the men of her city shall stone her with stones that she die: because she hath wrought folly in Israel, to play the whore in her father's house: so shalt thou put evil away from among you. (Deuteronomy 22:20–21)

If the accusation was untrue, the judgment could fall upon the man.

And, lo, he hath given occasions of speech against her, saying, I found not thy daughter a maid; and yet these are the tokens of my daughter's virginity. And they shall spread the cloth before the elders of the city. And the elders of that city shall take that man and chastise him; And they shall amerce him in an hundred shekels of silver, and give them unto the father of the damsel, because he hath brought up an evil name upon a virgin of Israel: and she shall be his wife; he may not put her away all his days. (Deuteronomy 22:17–19)

This scenario doesn't sound promising either way up to this point. That is why elders of the gate were to be men in whom the spirit of God dwelled. They were to be men who really walked with God, so God could reveal information to them by way of his spiritual connection for the purpose of bringing deliverance to all involved parties.

Although God's thoughts and will are expressed throughout the verses in the Bible, God's thoughts extend beyond the written Scriptures. There are not enough words to articulate the expanse of his thoughts, or books to contain His will, because God fills all eternity! 1 Corinthians 2:9 breathtakingly states, "But as it is written, Eye hath not seen, nor ear heard, neither have entered into the heart of man, the things which God hath prepared for them that love him." God can communicate [by revelation] through his spiritual connection in a man or a woman, that which might not otherwise come up in one's mind or heart.

The written Scriptures are vital because they provide the checks and balances to authenticate revelation. The details and applications given by revelation are specific for a particular situation, person, or persons. What God reveals to do in one situation may not be appropriate in a similar situation. God is that personalized! When men and women walk by the spirit of God, his heart of goodness and deliverance will be evident for each individual need.

The record of Joseph and Mary is a clear indication of God's great goodness, and love.

> *Now the birth of Jesus Christ was on this wise: When as his mother Mary was espoused [during the ten-day wedding ceremony] to Joseph, before they came together [had sexual relations], she was found with child of the Holy Ghost. Then Joseph her husband, being a just man, and not willing to make her a publick example, was minded to put her away privily [privately]. But while he thought on these things, behold, the angel of the Lord appeared unto him in a dream [vision], saying, Joseph, thou son of David, fear not to take unto thee Mary thy wife: for that which is conceived in her is of the Holy Ghost. (Matthew 1:18–20)*

Based solely on what is written, it appears Joseph had only two scriptural options; have Mary stoned, according to Deuteronomy 22, or write her a bill of divorcement.

> *When a man hath taken a wife, and married her, and it come to pass that she find no favor in his eyes, because he hath found some uncleanness in her: then let him write her a bill of divorcement, and give it in her hand, and send her out of his house. (Deuteronomy 24:1)*

The options in life are not that confined and neither is the will of God to deliver his people. Suppose the man didn't hate his wife? Suppose she still found favor in his eyes? What then? An observer, looking at these verses and Mary's pregnant condition could formulate one judgment; but God, looking upon both Joseph's and Mary's hearts, had a solution to this dilemma—a third option. Could Mary still have given birth to Jesus if

Joseph divorced her? Sure; but obviously, they wanted to be married. God does not disrupt their lives to accomplish salvation for mankind. Rather, he blesses their lives.

The record goes on to work out the details that were apparently satisfactory for Mary and Joseph. They not only enjoyed their marriage and raised their own children; they were entrusted to be the earthly parents of God's only begotten Son. God's wisdom continues to bring deliverance beyond what is written, as described in the following verses.

> *Now unto him that is able to do exceeding abundantly above all that we ask or think, according to the power that worketh in us. (Ephesians 3:20)*

> *But the wisdom that is from above is first pure [uncontaminated by evil], then peaceable, gentle [suitable, fit; not insisting on the letter of the law[4]], and easy to be entreated, full of mercy and good fruits, without partiality, and without hypocrisy. (James 3:17)*

Look how tenderly and lovingly God will respond to our needs. There is so much grace, mercy, and comfort in his communications. It is not the letter of the law he insists upon, but that good fruits may abound.

Many of the scribes and Pharisees regarded the Scriptures as a linguistic holy exercise for the scholarly and the intellectual. These high-minded ones placed themselves above their brethren. Cloaked in self-righteousness, they viewed the "common Israelites" as willful sinners, undeserving of compassion. They reasoned that the woes and subjugation of Israel to foreign forces had to have come upon them because of these "sinful ones." In judging their brethren, they became critical and hard of heart.

Rather than to allow the spirit of God to work in them to relieve those in need, these misguided ministers and leaders, through their egotism and position, were influenced by Satan to impose even heavier burdens upon the people of God. They selfishly utilized God's words to insulate themselves from the heart cries of their brethren.

Saying, The scribes and the Pharisees sit in Moses' seat: All therefore whatsoever they bid you observe, that observe and do; but do not ye after their works: for they say, and do not. For they bind heavy burdens and grievous to be borne, and lay them on men's shoulders; but they themselves will not move them with one of their fingers. (Matthew 23:2–4)

Woe unto you, scribes and Pharisees, hypocrites! for ye pay tithe of mint and anise and cummin, and have omitted the weightier matters of the law, judgment, mercy, and faith [believing]: these ought ye to have done, and not to leave the other undone. (Matthew 23:23)

Others of these elders were deceived by Satan through elevating religious ritual and the commandments added by men above the commandments of God. Upholding and fulfilling the traditions and ordinances of men became their focus. These elders measured their righteousness by exercising their power over the lives of people, rather than their own exercising of God's power in the people's lives.

Then the Pharisees and the scribes asked him, Why walk not thy disciples according to the tradition of the elders, but eat bread with unwashen hands? He answered and said unto them, Well hath Esaias prophesied of you hypocrites, as it is written, This people honoureth me with their lips, but their heart is far from me. Howbeit in vain do they worship me, teaching for doctrines the commandments of men? For laying aside the commandment of God, ye hold the tradition of men, as the washing of pots and cups: and many other such like things ye do. And he said unto them, Full well ye reject the commandment of God, that ye may keep your own tradition. (Mark 7:5–9)

Allegiances to commandments imposed by the will of men and man-made traditions deteriorated their effectiveness to really attend to the things of God: judgment, mercy, and believing. Hence, the warning, "Beware lest any man spoil you through philosophy and vain deceit, after the tradition of men, after the rudiments of the world, and not after Christ (Colossians 2:8)."

Judging whether God's people were acting within their prescribed liturgy became more essential than the reason God called them. Satan seduced these leaders and ministers to work against the very God they were to serve with all their hearts and the people whom they were to love as themselves. Clearly, these leaders, from among whom the elders of the gate were chosen, could not supply the need for equity and mercy.

Were these leaders, worshippers? Certainly, but the Scriptures identify them as vain worshippers. God sent Jesus Christ to reach mankind and make him righteous through belief in his Son. Yet through the rituals of ordinances, ceremonies and traditions, the scribes and Pharisees endeavored to attain to the righteousness of God.

In carrying out the will of his Father, Jesus Christ endeavored to break men free from these religious traditions and commandments. Jesus Christ provided a way out for even the most devoutly trained, if he or she has an ear to hear and a heart to believe. How loving God and his Son are, to work to redeem even those of us who may have inadvertently worshipped in vain.

The story of Nicodemus is an example.

> *There was a man of the Pharisees, named Nicodemus, a ruler of the Jews: The same came to Jesus by night, and said unto him, Rabbi, we know that thou art a teacher come from God: for no man can do these miracles that thou doest, except God be with him. Jesus answered and said unto him, Verily, verily, I say unto thee, Except a man be born again [born from above], he cannot see the kingdom of God. (John 3:1–3)*

Wouldn't you agree that Nicodemus's coming to Jesus indicates he is seeing something about the kingdom of God? He recognizes the miracles and acknowledges that they are from God. Jesus responds by encouraging Nicodemus:

Verily, verily, I say unto thee, We speak that we do know, and testify that we have seen; and ye receive not our witness [to listen in agreement, but not apply the lessons taught]. (John 3:11)

Notice Jesus did not say Nicodemus did not believe the testimony of his disciples. He is telling Nicodemus that he is not evidencing the same power (signs, miracles, and wonders) Jesus' other disciples were performing and manifesting. Surely, as a ruler of God's people, Nicodemus would want to do more than talk about God and the Scriptures. Wouldn't he want to use the power of God to meet the tremendous needs of men and women? Jesus is encouraging Nicodemus to break out of the mold and entanglements caused by the commandments of men and be a faithful minister.

Jesus used the example of the serpent of brass God had Moses make for the children of Israel when the fiery serpents came among them and bit them (Numbers 21 and Deuteronomy 8). It was placed upon a pole to be above all the priests, the rulers, the princes, and all men of influence.

And as Moses lifted up the serpent in the wilderness, even so must the Son of man be lifted up: That whosoever believeth in him should not perish, but have eternal life. (John 3:14–15)

If those bitten looked to the brass serpent Moses held aloft, they would live. If their focus remained on the level of men, no matter their position, stature, or influence, there would be no deliverance. As with most items fashioned from the senses realm, the people began to revere the relic rather than the power of God it was to signify. During the reign of Hezekiah, king of Judah, he destroyed this point of contact because it had become a religious icon.

He removed the high places, and brake the images, and cut down the groves, and brake in pieces the brazen serpent that Moses had made: for unto those days the children of Israel did burn incense to it: and he called it Nehushtan [a piece of brass]. He trusted in the Lord God of Israel; so that after him was none like him among all the kings of Judah, nor any that were before him. For he clave to the Lord, and departed not from following him, but kept his commandments, which the Lord commanded Moses. (2 Kings 18:4–6)

Jesus challenged Nicodemus, a ruler, leader, and master teacher of God's people, to hold aloft Christ for the people, not commandments of men and rituals that undermined God's power. Nicodemus could have taught the words of true deliverance that would have set them free, equipping them to receive and experience the power of God unobstructed.

For God so loved the world, that he gave his only begotten Son, that whosoever believeth in him should not perish, but have everlasting life. For God sent not his Son into the world to condemn the world; but that the world through him might be saved [made whole]. (John 3:16–17)

What commandment of men in the whole world has sent a savior for mankind? What tradition has dispatched a redeemer for humanity? Commandments of men demand the individual, through self-purification and self-sacrifice, perhaps even martyrdom, to save himself. Jesus Christ was and is God's magnanimous plan to save the world.

Did Nicodemus ever really break free of this dogma to become the man he was called to be? He certainly appreciated Jesus, but apparently did not rise above ceremony. Nicodemus prepared Jesus' body for burial according to tradition, which was unnecessary because God raised Jesus from the grave. I'm sure he'll have eternity to enjoy the benefits of God, but as a master teacher for Israel, he could have enjoyed much more in this life. He missed the blessing of bringing light to those who sat in darkness.

Some religious training is very difficult to overcome. Yet the Apostle Paul was able to rise above his upbringing and religious indoctrination to fulfill God's call for his life.

Circumcised the eighth day, of the stock of Israel, of the tribe of Benjamin, an Hebrew of Hebrews; as touching the law, a Pharisee; But what things were gain to me, those I counted loss for Christ. Yea doubtless, and I count all things but loss for the excellency of the knowledge of Christ Jesus my Lord: for whom I have suffered the loss of all things, and do count them but dung, that I may win Christ. (Philippians 3:5, 7–8)

Men and women will not find true justice in a civil legal system that does not regard spiritual matters. Neither is deliverance found through religious tradition and ritual. At best, legal systems can assign guilt and devise punishment for the sinner. As in most cultures, because of traditions and customs, people are often treated more callously by religious leaders than by the civil authority. Only through God's love in Christ can we rise above familial traditions, ethnical biases, racial prejudices, religious superstitions, tribal customs, and cultural taboos to enjoy the fullness of joy God intended for mankind.

◆　　　◆　　　◆

I have always found that mercy bears richer fruits than strict justice.

—Abraham Lincoln

◆　　　◆　　　◆

There is a real tenderness within the will of God and he is full of mercies and compassions for the weaknesses in men and women. The elders of the gate were to recognize these frailties and administer the word to bring restoration and healing.

And the scribes and Pharisees brought unto him a woman taken in adultery; and when they had set her in the midst, They say unto him, Master, this woman was taken in adultery, in the very act. Now Moses in the law commanded us, that such should be stoned: but what sayest thou? This they said, tempting him, that they might have to accuse him. But Jesus stooped down, and with his finger wrote on the ground, as though he heard them not. *(John 8:3–6)*

The original words used in the phrase "in the very act," actually indicate that she had confessed this act to the scribes and Pharisees; however, they exploited her personal and private contrition in order to assault Jesus.

The concern of the scribes and Pharisees was not for this woman's heart, nor for the will of God to prevail. They hatched a foolproof plan in an attempt to discredit Jesus. If Jesus told them to let her go, they would accuse him of not observing the Law of Moses, and therefore he would be considered a false prophet. If Jesus said she should be stoned, they would claim he was so unmerciful and could not possibly be the awaited messiah of God. The "perfect" trap was set.

So when they continued asking him, he lifted up himself, and said unto them, He that is without sin among you, let him first cast a stone at her. And again he stooped down, and wrote on the ground. (John 8:7–8)

Jesus focused his mind and heart to seek the proper intent of the Scriptures. By revelation to him from the Almighty, the heavenly Father revealed the perfect answer that brought deliverance from this satanic attack upon Jesus and the woman. Jesus answered them, "He that is without sin among you, let him first cast a stone at her."

And they which heard it, *being convicted by* their own *conscience, went out one by one, beginning at the eldest,* even *unto the last: and Jesus was left alone, and the woman standing in the midst. When Jesus had lifted up himself, and saw none but the woman, he said unto her, Woman, where are those thine accusers? hath no man condemned thee? She said, No man, Lord. And Jesus said unto her, Neither do I condemn thee: go, and sin no more. (John 8:9–11)*

Certainly the office of an elder of the gate was to be a highly respected position in the community. This regency was delegated for good and for the advancement of God's people: spiritually, morally, and even economically.

The book of Proverbs contains sayings to make a young man wise and is a companion to the Song of Solomon. In Proverbs, there are two women; the strange woman and the virtuous woman. The strange woman represents the seduction of earthly wisdom (earthly, sensual, and devilish), the wisdom that is so appealing to the senses. The virtuous woman represents that wisdom which is from above. The virtuous woman, as a wife and helpmeet, brings out the best in her husband. "Her husband is known in the gates, when he sitteth among the elders of the land" (Proverbs 31:23). The point is that the best companion to a leader of God's people is the wisdom of God. It is the helpmeet to bring out the best service to the people of God.

Jesus, with his life, modeled the work of an elder of the gate. His concern was for the truth of God's word and its proper application to bring deliverance and justice.

CHAPTER IV:
THE DAYSMAN

In the Bible lands a third forum looked to for settling disputes or claims, was the "daysman."[1] The daysman was the most renowned and wisest elder of the village. He was not elected by the people nor appointed by the authorities. Rather, he became recognized for the spiritual quality of his life as he grew up in his village. Usually, he was a man of wealth—first spiritually, then ethically, morally, intellectually, and financially. He was loved and revered by the entire village because he was an advocate for all. His intent was for the benefit and advancement of the whole community by elevating all the parts.

The word *daysman* comes from the Latin *diem dicere*, meaning to fix a day for hearing or cause. A day was set to appear before the daysman to hear the dispute or claim by the parties involved. The quarreling parties would sit on either side of the daysman and tell their story, each in turn. The daysman would listen intently to each one.

One may have loaned the other money for an emergency medical situation, and that one failed to repay. Maybe the lender became fearful that a need would arise in his life, and he would not have the funds necessary. He worried that his need would go unmet.

The borrower might be afraid and embarrassed because he did not have the money to repay on time and would try to avoid his friend. He may have grown defensive about the honor of his intentions to repay the loan.

After each side presented their case, the daysman, with great love, would open the scrolls; and, beginning with all parties' mutual love for the truth, would help them to overcome their fears and restore their trust in the Almighty. Through the teaching of the Scriptures, he would dispel the darkness that had obscured their vision of the truth, where unbelief had stealthily come in to steal the joys of the fellowship they had with the Father and with each other. The daysman would confront each one's wrong thinking by showing them, through the Scriptures, how God was good, generous, and would not neglect or forget their need.

Through the daysman's teaching, the borrower would recognize the great love God had stirred in the lender's heart to show compassion for his need and his true selflessness to assist him. Instead of appearing before the daysman, the lender could have had him imprisoned. The borrower would become repentant for his fear and would determine in his heart to trust God and work diligently to repay with the same love and attitude that was demonstrated toward his welfare.

The lender would realize that God had done great things for him and had provided that surplus to have the blessedness of helping his neighbor in his time of necessity (Acts 20:35; Ephesians 4:28). He would be thankful that his confidence for God's abundant supply allowed him to be a part in the healing of his neighbor.

The daysman would pray for them and place his hand on each man, signifying the presence and power of God upon their lives for blessing and healing. Both parties would weep and fall at each other's feet, kissing them, until forgiveness would be granted. The kissing of the feet was an Eastern expression of confession and desire for reconciliation.

Then the daysman would remind the borrower of his duty to repay the loan. The borrower might tell the daysman that he has no money at this time but promise to repay the debt. The daysman, out of his own abundance, might redeem the borrower by providing full payment and settling the debt. He might then tell the borrower, "This day you have been redeemed."

The daysman would then provide the parties with something to eat containing salt. The salt represented a covenant of absolute commitment to their words. Salted words are referenced in Colossians 4:6, "Let your speech *be* alway with grace, seasoned with salt, that ye may know how ye ought to answer every man."

The covenant was that the offense would never be repeated. The matter would be considered closed, and they would conduct their lives as if the incident never took place. Both parties would be free to go on their way, restored and whole. The village therefore was blessed to receive the two strong souls, who, in turn, would strengthen others.

Situations in life are not always simple. The requirement for deeper spiritual understanding and power are essential for mankind to live in peace. There are great spiritual forces underlying and controlling life's events. The man of the flesh, and even the senses-minded "Christian" (born again but lacking in spiritual understanding), measures and evaluates life limited to the five senses. They may talk about Satan and satanic attacks, but in actuality they fix their blame, and thus their retribution, upon other people, never approaching the root cause. One group of men may refer to the other as an "axis of evil." The other group echoes, "The great Satan." In reality, the evil spirit realm has done a pretty good job convincing the world that man is Satan, when actually; our conflict is spiritual in nature.

For we wrestle not against flesh and blood, but against principalities, against powers, against the rulers of the darkness of this world, against spiritual wickedness in high places. (Ephesians 6:12)

Some versions of this passage read "wicked spirits from on high." These wicked spirits are the ardent enemies of God, the people of God, and indeed, mankind as a whole. That is why the complete annihilation of a people or groups of people will never eradicate evil because its roots are spiritual. Satan will simply move in another group or another form.

This evil spirit realm underlies the addictions and perversions in our world. They foment and promote insanity, murders, and the like, that have plagued mankind from the days of Cain. Through possession, coercion, and torment they have ruled the souls of men and women and disfigured humanity by their tyranny. That is not to say that there are not evil men and women who freely lend their bodies and minds to this malicious spirit realm.

Since God is spirit and mankind is flesh, men and women needed a means of contact with God within that would remain unbroken or uninterrupted (John 3:6; Romans 8:4). The Old Testament promised that the coming redeemer would be the daysman; that is, he would be the mediator between God (who is Spirit) and man (who is flesh), an intercessor against Satan's attacks.

The book of Job aptly illustrates mankind's dilemma, verifying the need for this intermediary. Among it pages, it is no small wonder that the grand need for a daysman would be so pronounced. Job was well aware of this promised daysman; however, he knew that this need had not yet been fulfilled, "Neither is there any daysman betwixt us, *that* might lay his hand upon us both" (Job 9:33).

The Book of Job begins with God's declaration of his desire for mankind mirrored in the life of Job. It starts with Job being a man of great prosperity, fruitful in his family life and personal relationships when Satan comes on the scene to disrupt all the blessings with which God had blessed Job.

Biblically, the term *Satan* is used in reference to how mankind's spiritual adversaries (the devil and the whole evil spirit realm) exercise their influence in the world through nations, people, circumstances, conditions, philosophies, religions, and even biologically and environmentally, to attack humanity. They seek to prey upon fears to bring about harm and loss. Satan is pitiless and attacks without provocation. Isaiah 14:6 expresses, "He who smote the people in wrath with a continual stroke, he that ruled the nations in anger, is persecuted, *and* none hindereth." The Aramaic translation reads "he [Satan] persecuted them without pity."

Job 2:7 says, "So went Satan forth from the presence of the Lord, and smote Job with sore boils from the sole of his foot unto his crown." Who smote Job with sickness and injury? Satan did! All the calamity that came upon Job and his family was through the workings of Satan. Satan moved through people and the environment (meteorologically as well as biologically), to exert this attack against Job and his family.

When God re-established the earth in Genesis, he set many laws in nature. These natural laws provide for the earth to care for itself, so to speak. For instance, he ordered the transition of seasons, general periods of temperature to allow crops to be planted, grown, and harvested. He set rules for the tides and their limits upon the shores (Proverbs 8:29).

God in his goodness provided an order to these things to bless all of mankind (Matthew 5:45). These natural laws of God continue to govern today. However, when certain meteorological or biological conditions exist, Satan, as the god of this world (2 Corinthians 4:4), can take advantage of these circumstances to bring about "natural phenomenon" or so-called "acts of God," for example storms, floods, earthquakes, outbreaks of disease, and plagues. Similarly, in the exercise of the true God's spiritual power, genuine phenomenon have occurred to deliver God's people or to restore order, such as the parting of the Red Sea and Jesus calming the storm.

In his wisdom, God instituted laws of life such as free will and laws which govern faith, in order to offer salvation on the simplest plane for anyone to accept. When applied properly, these laws bear great fruit. Conversely, if applied wrongly, they do not bear the anticipated fruit or benefit. The antithetical spirit world works overtime to influence people to choose the wrong application.

God's will for man is health and prosperity, "Beloved, I wish above all things that thou mayest prosper and be in health, even as thy soul prospereth" (3 John 2). Another acknowledgment of God's will concerning prosperity can be read in Psalms:

Let them shout for joy, and be glad, that favor my righteous cause: yea, let them say continually, Let the Lord be magnified, which hath pleasure in the prosperity of his servant. (Psalms 35:27)

God has written abundance into the very fabric of life. His goodness is so great. When his order is allowed to flow uninterrupted, even the unbelieving are blessed, as set forth in the Gospels:

That ye may be the children of your Father which is in heaven: for he maketh his sun to rise on the evil and on the good, and sendeth rain on the just and on the unjust. (Matthew 5:45)

Perhaps you have read this verse and thought of the term *maketh his sun* as something good and *sendeth rain* as something negative; sort of like the expression, "taking the good with the bad." That is not the meaning at all.

The word translated *rain* is used only of a gentle drizzle to facilitate growth, like the "former rain" and the "latter rain" associated with a bountiful planting season and harvest. When the Scriptures talk about severe rainstorms, a different word is translated "rain." Once again, we see that God is good always!

Satan is also called "the accuser of our brethren."

And I heard a loud voice saying in heaven, Now is come salvation, and strength, and the kingdom of our God, and the power of his Christ: for the accuser of our brethren is cast down, which accused them before our God day and night. And they overcame him by the blood of the Lamb, and by the word of their testimony; and they loved not their lives unto the death. (Revelation 12:10–11)

Who would stand on Job's behalf? Who would declare the truth to Job under Satan's unprovoked attacks? Job desperately needed a daysman to intercede on his behalf. He needed to be reminded of the blessedness and healing he had in the presence of God. Job said, "For the thing which I greatly feared is come upon me, and that which I was afraid of is come unto me" (Job 3:25).

Many people stop here and identify with Job's plight and difficult circumstances. Who has not been touched with the negatives and injuries of this life? However, our identification is in Christ and in God's deliverance.

Job knew he needed someone who would quell his fear. He needed to be reminded of God's thoughts toward him. He needed to be comforted by the power and presence of God. Job needed someone to intercede, to be his daysman.

The Hebrew word for *daysman* is *yakach* (pronounced *yaw'—kahh*). A great revealing truth to its meaning is found in Isaiah 1:18, which says:

> *Come now, and let us reason together [yakach], saith the Lord: though your sins be as scarlet, they shall be as white as snow; though they be red like crimson, they shall be as wool.*

The aim of doing the work of a daysman is to bring about pardon and redemption. It is to give a fresh start and a cleansing from unrighteousness, as described in the following verses.

> *If we confess our sins, he is faithful and just to forgive us our sins, and to cleanse us from all unrighteousness. (1 John 1:9)*

> *My little children, these things write I unto you, that ye sin not. And [But] if any man sin, we have an advocate with the Father, Jesus Christ the righteous: And he is the propitiation [full payment in place and on behalf of] for our sins: and not for ours only, but also for the sins of the whole world. (1 John 2:1–2)*

The record revolves around discourse between three of Job's friends and a fourth man, named Elihu. None of Job's three friends (Bildad, Eliphaz, or Zophar) were advocates for Job's cause. They were well-meaning perhaps, but they did not seek to heal his heart or quell his fears. With all their words and reasoning, they failed to restore Job's wonderful relationship with God.

These "friends" floated every conceivable possibility of hidden sins in Job's life, but none quoted back to him God's testimony of his life. Twice, God called Job "perfect and upright." Perhaps the words they did speak even retarded Job's believing for deliverance.

Elihu, reproved Job's friends for their ineffectual ministering to Job's need. "Yea, I attended unto you, and, behold, *there was* none of you that convinced [*yakach*] Job, *or* that answered his words (Job 32:12).

Unfortunately, Elihu behaved himself even more unbecomingly to Job than Bildad, Eliphaz, and Zophar put together. His verbose philosophical ramblings go on for six chapters. Although he speaks some truth, it is mostly "couched" to inflate his own ego.

> *Wherefore, Job, I pray thee, hear my speeches, and hearken to all my words. Behold, now I have opened my mouth, my tongue hath spoken in my mouth. My words shall be of the uprightness of my heart: and my lips shall utter knowledge clearly. Behold, I am according to thy wish in God's stead: I also am formed out of the clay. (Job 33:1–3, 6)*

It appears that Elihu thought that he was indeed the promised daysman. However, when he finally does finish speaking, God's assessment of Elihu in Job 38:1–2 is not so flattering: "Then the Lord answered Job out of the whirlwind, and said, Who *is* this that darkeneth counsel by words without knowledge?"

We shouldn't judge Job's friends too harshly, for Christ, the advocate and daysman for the world, had not yet come. The promise was not yet fulfilled.

It would be unjust to God not to complete the record of Job to show that God is indeed a deliverer and healer, for God "turned the captivity of Job, when he prayed for his friends: also the Lord gave Job twice as much as he had before" (Job 42:10).

The Lord turned away Job's captivity. He delivered Job from being led away as a prisoner. In addition, he gave to Job double of all that he had. Let's now go back and compare.

> *And there were born unto him [Job] seven sons and three daughters. His substance also was seven thousand sheep, and three thousand camels, and five hundred yoke of oxen, and five hundred she asses, and a very great household; so that this man was the greatest of all the men of the east. (Job 1:2–3)*

Job certainly had abundance to start with, didn't he? Now let us look at the last chapter in Job.

> *So the Lord blessed the latter end of Job more than his beginning: for he had fourteen thousand sheep, and six thousand camels, and a thousand yoke of oxen, and a thousand she asses. He had also seven sons and three daughters. (Job 42:12–13)*

In his beginning Job had 7,000 sheep; now he has 14,000. That's double the amount. He first had 3,000 camels; now they total 6,000. Twice as much! And 500 yoke of oxen increased to 1,000 yoke, with 500 she asses that are now 1,000. A twofold increase just as verse 10 expounded!

Then verse 13 declares that Job "had also seven sons and three daughters." How many did Job have at the beginning? Job 1:2 says: "And there were born unto him seven sons and three daughters."

Something is wrong. Didn't the Scriptures tell us that "the Lord gave Job twice as much as he had before"? Yet he only has seven sons and three daughters.

The "latter end" of Job includes the resurrection of the just. At that time Job and his wife will spend all of eternity with their fourteen sons and six daughters—double, just as the Scriptures declared. How wonderful our God is and how accurate is his word. As Romans 11:33 says, "O the depth of the riches both of the wisdom and knowledge of God! how unsearchable *are* his judgments, and his ways past finding out!"

CHAPTER V:
THE PROMISED DAYSMAN

In the New Testament the word for *daysman* is "mediator: one in the middle who settles and reconciles by intervening as a peacemaker."[1] The following verses describe this role:

> *For* there is *one God, and one mediator between God and men, the man Christ Jesus; Who gave himself a ransom for all, to be testified in due time. (1 Timothy 2:5–6)*

> *Wherefore he is able also to save them to the uttermost that come unto God by him, seeing he ever liveth to make intercession for them. (Hebrews 7:25)*

Isn't it fortifying to know that we have Christ Jesus our Lord making intercession for us? When Satan, the great accuser of God's people, is present, bringing accusations against us, trying to tear at us, and slander our good reputations; Christ Jesus is there at the right hand of God, interceding against Satan and for us. As it says in Romans 8:34, "Who *is* he that condemneth? *It is* Christ that died, yea rather, that is risen again, who is even at the right hand of God, who also maketh intercession for us."

The words *it is* are not in the text. The two sentences are actually rhetorical questions. With all that Christ did for us in his death, resurrection, and ascension, is he now, while seated at the right hand of God, going to be whispering condemnations of us in God's ear? That would be preposterous. Is he going to be agreeing with Satan against us? How ridiculous!

Who will stand for us in our hour of need? Why, Christ of course. He is our advocate against Satan's slander. He is our defense attorney. He reminds Satan of God's testimony concerning us. It is the spirit of God in Christ in us that works to encourage us to will and to do God's good pleasure.

> *According as he [God] hath chosen us in him [Christ] before the foundation of the world, that we should be holy and without blame before him [God] in love: To the praise of the glory of his grace, wherein he hath made us accepted in the beloved [with the beloved ones]. (Ephesians 1:4, 6)*

> *And you [Even you], that were sometime alienated and enemies in your mind by wicked works, yet now hath he [God in Christ] reconciled. In the body of his [Jesus Christ's] flesh through death, to present you holy and unblameable [without stain or blemish[2]] and unreproveable [though blamed, yet undeserving of blame[3]] in his [God's] sight. (Colossians 1:21–22)*

Can you see why Job longed for the daysman; why he desired to have him "lay his hand upon us both"? What God has done for us in Christ gives us the legal basis for true justice against Satan who continues to foment evil against mankind and to rob humanity from the blessedness of the power and presence of God!

Jesus Christ of Nazareth, the Son of God, was and is the daysman for mankind. He is the elder of the gate, our redeemer, and savior. It is in his wonderful name that blessedness and wholeness are restored in the power and presence of God. By confessing Jesus as Lord and by believing God raised him from the dead, we are saved. That is how we are born into the mighty family of God. Let's read Romans 10:9:

> *That if thou shalt confess with thy mouth the Lord Jesus, and shalt believe in thine heart that God hath raised him from the dead, thou shalt be saved.*

By our careful study of the Scriptures, we can know who we are and what we have in Christ Jesus. As we live in the light of his triumph over Satan, we will live in victory over the spirit realm that intends to defeat our lives.

> *Study to shew thyself approved unto God, a workman that needeth not to be ashamed, rightly dividing the word of truth. (2 Timothy 2:15)*

> *Nay, in all these things we are more than conquerors through him that loved us. For I am persuaded, that neither death, nor life, nor angels, nor principalities, nor powers, nor things present, nor things to come, Nor height, nor depth, nor any other creature, shall be able to separate us from the love of God, which is in Christ Jesus our Lord. (Romans 8:37–39)*

Still, there will be men and women who do not believe the inspiring report and witness concerning Jesus, who is the Christ, the savior for the world. Through Satan's deceptions and the weaknesses in man, many will not choose the holy one of God, as explained in Mark 16:16: "He that believeth and is baptized [totally immersed in all that his name represents] shall be saved; but he that believeth not shall be damned."

Most scholarly writings that I have read on this subject agree that this unbeliever is damned; that is, God has condemned him to hell. However, the word translated *damned* in this verse means to hand down judgment against. The questions arise: Who is doing the judging at this point? And what is the judgment?

A key to unlocking this verse is in our overall scope of the Scripture and our understanding that God is merciful and all light. The Bible tells us in 1 Corinthians 4:3 that today is "man's day," that is, the day and time in which man does the judging: "But with me it is a very small thing that I should be judged of you, or of man's judgment: yea, I judge not mine own self."

Some Bibles with study helps make note that *man's judgment* should read, "man's day." Today is when man hands down the judgments against others and even himself. In this case, the one judging is "he that believeth not." Who is he judging or handing down judgment against? He is passing judgment upon himself. The words translated from the Greek text as *believeth not* refer to one who has not listened long enough to hear, and therefore not made the choice to believe.

The word translated *saved* means wholeness. He that believeth not has judged himself unworthy of wholeness, and therefore does not allow himself to hear enough to believe. He does not recognize the accomplishments of Christ's death, resurrection, and ascension, and judges himself unworthy to enjoy those things in this life that come with eternal life.

Paul faced a similar situation in Antioch of Pisidia while ministering there. Some of the Jews, envious of the crowds gathering to hear Paul and Barnabas, contradicted the words Paul spoke.

> *Then Paul and Barnabas waxed bold, and said, It was necessary that the word of God should first have been spoken to you: but seeing ye put it from you, and judge yourselves unworthy of everlasting life, lo, we turn to the Gentiles. (Acts 13:46)*

Paul and Barnabas were extremely desirous for these Jews to receive the testimony and manifest the power of God in the name of Jesus Christ. They wanted them to make use of those things pertaining to eternal life. However, in their unbelieving hearts, those Jews judged themselves unworthy to experience the power of the world to come, not believing on the only begotten Son of God.

Could these unbelieving Jews heal the sick in the name of Jesus Christ? Could they raise the dead in Christ's name? No! Why? Because they did not believe his name carried power or worth. They judged themselves unworthy of Jesus Christ's accomplishments for mankind.

At the proper time, God will issue his ultimate judgment. His judgment will trump the judgment of man's day, and the power of the Lord's Day will bring his deliverance, unhindered by unbelief.

What day is today? This period is called man's day, But there is a day coming, called the Lord's Day, when he will hand down judgments. In that appointed day, all man's judgments will be superseded by the judgment of God. When the Lord does the judging, he will not look on the outward appearance, but upon the hearts of men and women. In that brilliant day, when Satan will not be able to pervert the gospel or deceive the people, those who have denied themselves victory in Christ in this life will have the option of making their choice in the crystal-clear, luminous light of the truth. Then, the man or woman of unbelief will undoubtedly hear enough and see enough to choose Christ and restructure their destiny.

For those who do believe, this triumph in Christ can be experienced and enjoyed right now, even while it is man's day. In this life, we can have the wholeness and fullness of joy, walking with the Father, walking in the light.

Verily, verily, I say unto you, He that heareth my word, and believeth on him that sent me, hath everlasting life, and shall not come into condemnation; but is passed from death unto life. (John 5:24)

These things have I written unto you that believe on the name of the Son of God; that ye may know that ye have eternal life, and that ye may believe on the name of the Son of God. (1 John 5:13)

From God's perspective, because of his foreknowledge, it is eternal life. To God, it has always existed. For man, because he recognizes a starting point when he was born again, in his understanding, it computes as everlasting life. Either way, it is the right of believing ones' to enjoy the benefits of eternal life, beginning now.

Why would anyone want to pass up the joy of walking with God in this life? When you truly understand how good God is and the blessings of walking with him, why wait for the future? Let your everlasting life start today!

◆   ◆   ◆

The only limit to our realization of tomorrow will be our doubts of today. Let us move forward with strong and active faith.

—Franklin D. Roosevelt

◆   ◆   ◆

CHAPTER VI:
THE PIVOTAL DAY FOR MANKIND

And when the day of Pentecost was fully come, they were all with one accord in one place. And suddenly there came a sound from heaven as of a rushing mighty wind, and it filled all the house where they were sitting. And there appeared unto them cloven tongues like as of fire, and it sat upon each of them. And they were all filled with the Holy Ghost [holy spirit], and began to speak with other tongues, as the Spirit gave them utterance. (Acts 2:1–4)

The Day of Pentecost chronicled in the second chapter of the book of Acts remains the pivotal day for mankind. It was on this particular Pentecost day that the promise of the Father arrived, substantiated by the outpouring of God's gift of holy spirit within for the first time. This outpouring far surpassed Moses' desire stated in Numbers 11:29, "Would God that all the Lord's people were prophets *and* that the Lord would put his spirit upon them!"

The new birth had arrived bringing God's gift of holy spirit within, never to be lost or forfeited. 1 Peter 1:23 describes it, "Being born again, not of corruptible seed, but of incorruptible, by the word of God, which liveth and abideth forever." The gospel of Luke calls it "the promise of my Father" and explains it to be "endued [clothed] with power from on high" (Luke 24:49). In the gospel of John, the gift of holy spirit is expressed as "the Comforter," "the Holy Ghost," "the Spirit of truth," and "born again" (John 14:26; 16:13; 3:7). Acts 1:5 characterizes it as "baptized with the Holy Ghost [holy spirit]" and Colossians 1:27 makes clear that it is "Christ in you, the hope of glory."

It is the gift of eternal life and the power of God within man. All the ability of Christ is given to the man or woman who believes on him. As Jesus spoke in John 14:12, "Verily, verily, I say unto you, He that believeth on me, the works that I do shall he do also; and greater *works* than these shall he do; because I go unto my Father."

Did Jesus go unto his Father? If the second part of this verse is true, surely, so must the first. If we are to do the works that Jesus did—and we are, then all the inherent assets and wisdom that accompany it must be available and ever present today. Jesus did not give an expiration date with this announcement!

Since that Day of Pentecost, everywhere there are believing men and women—there also, is the power of Christ. That is the reason 1Corinthians 2:7–9 exclaims:

> *But we speak the wisdom of God in a mystery,* even *the hidden* wisdom, *which God ordained before the world unto our glory: Which none of the princes of this world knew [the rulers of the evil spirit realm]: for had they known* it, *they would not have crucified the Lord of glory. But as it is written, Eye hath not seen, nor ear heard, neither have entered into the heart of man, the things which God hath prepared for them that love him.*

By crucifying our Lord, Satan made a grave error. Now unto everyone "that believeth on him," Christ is born within and the power of God is present to heal. The works that Jesus did we are to also do. 1 John 3:8 speaks loudly and clearly, "For this purpose the Son of God was manifested, that he might destroy the works of the devil." Satan's problem has increased exponentially.

Pentecost, the starting day of the Feast of the Firstfruits, means "a fiftieth."[1] It was the fiftieth day counting from the second day of Passover. Fifty has an association with the Year of Jubilee, which was the year of release (Leviticus 25 and 27; Numbers 36). In the fiftieth year debts were canceled, inheritances were returned, and slaves were freed. A new beginning, a fresh start was a great part in the lives of God's people.

On this Pentecost, pious men from every nation, every ethnical background had come to Jerusalem to attend this great feast as they had done in previous years. Yet, at this celebration, something astonishing and wonderful took place that shook the streets of Jerusalem. At about "the third hour of the day" these twelve Galileans began to manifest something so unusual it totally flabbergasted the onlookers leaving them dumbfounded and deeply perplexed because every man heard them in his own language speak "the wonderful works of God."

> And there were dwelling at Jerusalem Jews, devout men, out of every nation under heaven. Now when this was noised abroad, the multitude came together, and were confounded, because that every man heard them speak in his own language. And they were all amazed and marvelled, saying one to another, Behold, are not all these which speak Galilaeans? And how hear we every man in our own tongue, wherein we were born? Parthians, and Medes, and Elamites, and the dwellers in Mesopotamia, and in Judaea, and Cappadocia, in Pontus, and Asia, Phrygia, and Pamphylia, in Egypt, and in the parts of Libya about Cyrene, and strangers of Rome, Jews and proselytes, Cretes and Arabians, we do hear them speak in our tongues the wonderful works of God. (Acts 2:5–11)

This record in Acts 2 confirms the names of cities and regions from which these men had journeyed to attend the feast at Jerusalem. The twelve may have never traveled or perhaps never heard of some of these places, but God knew. These devout men wanted to know, "What meaneth this? (Acts 2:12)" In the midst of this phenomenal occurrence, no sooner was their attention and focus attracted, when "others" began to mock, accusing the twelve of being full of new wine (Acts 2:13).

But Peter, standing up with the eleven, lifted up his voice, and said unto them, Ye men of Judaea, and all ye that dwell at Jerusalem, be this known unto you, and hearken to my words: For these are not drunken, as ye suppose, seeing it is but the third hour of the day [around 9:00 a.m.]. But this is that which was spoken by the prophet Joel; And it shall come to pass in the last days, saith God, I will pour out of my Spirit [spirit, the gift of God] upon all flesh: and your sons and your daughters shall prophesy, and your young men shall see visions, and your old men shall dream dreams: And on my servants and on my handmaidens I will pour out in those days of my Spirit [spirit, the gift of God]; and they shall prophesy." (Acts 2:14–18)

In verse 16, *this* is in reference to the dynamic phenomenon they had just witnessed of the twelve apostles speaking the wonderful works of God in all these many languages, right down to the specific dialects. They were accustomed to hearing the glories of God expounded in Hebrew, and perhaps Aramaic, but hearing it in all these languages and dialects, including those of Gentile nations—they were shook! The mockers sought to disparage the importance and value of what God had wrought.

The word translated *pour* in verses 17 and 18, means to gush, pour out in abundance. This was not just a sprinkling of a drop or two. The idea is to be lavished joyfully. God was going to totally bathe them in his spirit. They were to be "baptized in the Holy Ghost;" that is, to be totally immersed in this gift of holy spirit.

The same word for *pour* is used in the *Septuagint* (the Greek translation of the Old Testament), in Malachi 3:10, "if I will not open you the windows of heaven, and pour you out a blessing, that *there shall* not *be room* enough *to receive it.*" How vast are the windows of heaven? In volume, it is inestimable.

In 2 Kings, Elisha asked for a "double portion" of the spirit that was upon Elijah. If you count the miracles under the ministry of Elisha you will find twice as many as those recorded of Elijah. On Pentecost, Peter quoting the Prophet Joel, said that God would "pour out" of his spirit.

Much bigger than a double portion, its magnitude and elegance cannot be fully expressed.

Remember, the promise was to be "endued (clothed) with power from on high." Perhaps to express wealth and luxury you might say "dripping with diamonds" or "wrapped in mink." It would not be merely a tentative drip. It would be plush, plush, plush! There would be honor, dignity, and respect associated with this clothing.

Being clothed with holds a deeper meaning than simply putting on clothing. Consider the record of Mordecai who uncovered a plot to assassinate King Ahasuerus (Esther 6:1–11). The king commanded that Mordecai be arrayed in his royal apparel, adorned with his crown, and set upon his royal steed to be paraded through the street of Shushan with the king's most noble princes proclaiming before him how the king delighted to honor Mordecai. Although these costly vestments and the steed were the property of the king, they represented the glory and power of the kingdom. Mordecai received the highest national honor. Arrayed in the king's clothing and wearing his crown signified glory, honor, and dignity. Riding upon the king's horse represented the enormous power of the kingdom at his disposal. Being paraded through the street of Shushan displayed unity and loyalty. Overall, the emphasis was on the abundance of benefits and resources for service to the kingdom.

On the Day of Pentecost, and every day since, believing ones are attired with all the honor, dignity, strength, and power of the kingdom of God. The rest of the book of Acts testifies to the many mighty works of the believing ones. From such overt, miraculous events as the healing of the man at the gate of the temple called Beautiful (Acts 3), to the magnificent healings and deliverances in Acts 5, which peaked with people bringing the sick and vexed for the shadow of Peter passing by to be cast over them. Tremendous deliverances are detailed in chapter 8 when Philip went to Samaria and Gaza. Miracles of healings and a woman raised from the dead in chapter nine. The powerful records continue chapter by chapter through to chapter twenty-eight. The records demonstrate the effectual workings of God's power in the lives and hearts of people from every quarter. When we add to the mix the subsequent events recorded throughout the church epistles, we see a vigorous church!

Were those believing ones faced with pressures and challenges? Yes, absolutely, right up to peril for their very lives. But in all things they proved themselves more than conquerors though him that loved them (Romans 8:37). We still live in the midst of a crooked and perverse world. Satan continues to attack with his scheming methods to discourage the righteous and dissuade the innocent. Let not your heart be troubled (John 14:1); remain strong in the Lord and in the power of his might (Ephesians 6:10). The Scriptures assure us "greater is he that is in you, than he that is in the world" (1 John 4:4).

We have been clothed with the same power that we too may get the things of God accomplished. God has fully equipped us so that we may be successful and bear much fruit. By the word of God and his spirit within he makes us able to every good work (2 Timothy 3:16–17). From a spiritual point of view we have everything we need to be like Christ and to walk in his steps.

We should seek from the Scriptures how this spirit from God is to work in us and how it is to be manifested so that we may produce this spiritual fruit. We indeed, should speak in tongues as a sign that we have received the power of his gift of holy spirit (Acts 2:11; 8:17; 10:46; 19:6), interpret tongues, and bring forth words of prophecy in our worship services decently and in order. We should evidence word of knowledge, word of wisdom, and discerning of spirits to bring forth spiritual solutions to the problems of our day and time, in keeping with the eternal truths abiding in the Scriptures. We should demonstrate the power of faith, miracles, and gifts of healing to bring deliverance from all the power of the enemy. The church is not weak but mighty to the pulling down of strongholds (2 Corinthians 10:4).

Our fleshly minds that have been conditioned to respond to our feelings and our fears will want to reject the freedom to live the love of Christ. The notion that the works he did we shall also do is absurd or even frightening but the equipment necessary is in place and the charge still stands: "But ye shall receive power, after that the Holy Ghost [holy spirit] is come upon you: and ye shall be witnesses unto me both in Jerusalem, and in all Judaea, and in Samaria, and unto the uttermost part of the earth" (Acts 1:8).

A *pivot* is a forward move to outmaneuver your opponent in a drive toward your goal. Pentecost in Acts chapter two was that day for the church. As living epistles, known and read of men, let our lives joyfully write Acts 29 and the subsequent chapters.

◆   ◆   ◆

The great use of life is to spend it on something that will outlast it.

—James Truslow Adams

◆   ◆   ◆

CHAPTER VII:
THE COMFORTER COMES

Neither academics nor cultural refinement will change the sinful nature of mankind. Men and women need the new birth, the gift of holy spirit from God born within them, to receive a new, diving nature. Then they can reckon themselves dead to sin, and alive to God through Christ.

> *According as his divine power hath given unto us all things that* per- tain *unto life and godliness, through the knowledge of him that hath called us to glory and virtue: Whereby are given unto us exceeding great and precious promises: that by these ye might be partakers of the divine nature, having escaped the corruption that is in the world through lust. (2 Peter 1:3–4)*

This spirit of God in an individual takes the place of the ascended Christ, now seated at the right hand of God. For that individual, the gift of holy spirit is the daysman and the promised comforter. What Jesus Christ did for humanity as he carried out his ministry to Israel, the spirit from God does in a man, woman, or child as they believe and go through life.

To receive this spirit of God is to be "clothed [endued] with power from on high" (Luke 29), which prepares us to be able witnesses. This is the promised comforter as explained in the following verses:

> *But ye shall receive power, after that the Holy Ghost [the gift from God] is come upon you: and ye shall be witnesses unto me both in Jerusalem, and in all Judaea, and in Samaria, and unto the uttermost part of the earth. (Acts 1:8)*

And I will pray the Father, and he shall give you another Comforter, that he may abide with you for ever; Even the Spirit [the gift from God] of truth; whom the world cannot receive, because it seeth him not, neither knoweth him: but ye know him; for he dwelleth with you, and shall be in you. I will not leave you comfortless; I will come to you. (John 14:16–18)

The word translated *comforter* means "one who is called alongside to give one aid."[1] In secular Greek writings it is used in reference to a legal assistant who may be called upon to provide help during a trial. That assistance particularly comes in the form of words of exhortation and edification, which result in comfort.

The spirit from God does not argue the case for us, but enables us to confidently declare the truth. This is not done before the "Bar of God" because that case was settled when we were justified and made righteous in Christ.

Nevertheless I tell you the truth; It is expedient for you that I go away: for if I go not away, the Comforter will not come unto you; but if I depart, I will send him unto you. And when he is come, he will reprove the world of sin, and of righteousness, and of judgment: Of sin, because they believe not on me; Of righteousness, because I go to my Father, and ye see me no more; Of judgment, because the prince of this world is judged. (John 16:7–11)

Our judgment is unto righteousness while the prince of this world is in all unrighteousness. Who is the great prince of this world? Satan and all the evil spirits that have troubled mankind are called "the rulers of the darkness of this world" (Ephesians 6:12). How revealing this evidence is to the spirit realm concerning Christ's victory over them and the glory of the witness we have within. At the same time it comforts us, as shown in the following verses:

And in nothing terrified by your adversaries: which is to them an evident token of perdition, but to you of salvation, and that of God. (Philippians 1:28)

But for us also, to whom it shall be imputed, if we believe on him that raised up Jesus our Lord from the dead; Who was delivered for our offenses, and was raised again for our justification. (Romans 4:24–25)

Therefore being justified by faith, we have peace with God through our Lord Jesus Christ: By whom also we have access by faith into this grace wherein we stand, and rejoice in hope of the glory of God. (Romans 5:1–2)

Our testimony and witness is in the "court of world opinion," so to speak. Our lives testify to the truth in 1 John 1:5 that "God is light and in him is no darkness at all." In the midst of Satan's slanderous attacks, evil inferences, and outright lies against our spiritual position before God, the spirit from God in us evidences that our names have truly been cleared through Christ's eminent name.

By the power of God in us, we demonstrate his genuine goodness, grace, and mercy to mankind. We speak the truth in love, reconciling men and women back to God so they too may partake of the healing power of his divine presence. In addition, we are to draw upon and use that power within to bring deliverance and release to those encased in fear, turning them from darkness to light.

As Paul wrote to the Church at Thessalonica:

For our gospel came not unto you in word only, but also in power, and in the Holy Ghost (the gift of God's spirit in man at the new birth), and in much assurance; as ye know what manner of men we were among you for your sake. (1 Thessalonians 1:5)

Our testimony and witness is given in a combination of words and works, not in word only. Paul said it best, "And my speech and my preaching *was* not with enticing words of man's wisdom, but in demonstration of the Spirit and of power" (1 Corinthians 2:4).

Jesus' exhortation in the gospel of John let them know there was something to accomplish once they received the promised comforter.

> *Verily, verily, I say unto you, He that believeth on me, the works that I do shall he do also; and greater works than these shall he do; because I go unto my Father. (John 14:12)*

Some of these works are set forth in the gospel of Mark just before Jesus' ascension. As the last recorded instructions of our Lord, we should take special heed to carry out his direction.

> *And he said unto them, Go ye into all the world, and preach the gospel [the good news] to every creature [to all creation]. He that believeth and is baptized shall be saved; but he that believeth not shall be damned. And these signs shall follow them that believe; In my name shall they cast out devils; they shall speak with new tongues; [If] They shall take up serpents; and if they shall drink any deadly thing, it shall not hurt them; they shall lay hands on the sick, and they shall recover. (Mark 16:15–18)*

As we look at the world around us, it is easy to see that with all of our social advancements and all of our technological breakthroughs, we fall woefully short to address the needs of mankind. The needs of humanity surpass scientific discovery and development, exceed the scope of nature, and reach beyond the helping hands of human kindness. Yet there beats the heart of a loving God who imparts to men and women his power to accomplish the impossible.

The record in Mark closes:

> *So then, after the Lord had spoken unto them, he was received up into heaven, and sat on the right hand of God. And they went forth, and*

preached every where, the Lord working with them, *and confirming the word with signs following. Amen.* (Mark 16:19–20)

The world is so in need of the children of God to continue the works begun in Christ. How much the world needs the goodness, mercy, and grace of God. How desperate the world is to be touched by the power of God. How can we know that we are ready or that we are truly prepared to carry out his direction?

If we receive the witness of men, the witness of God is greater: for this is the witness of God which he hath testified of his Son. He that believeth on the Son of God hath the witness in himself. (1 John 5:9–10)

Through the darkness of unbelief in this world, our testimony might be criticized, maligned, or just ignored. But the truth we live cannot be denied; it cannot be disproved.

For the eyes of the Lord are *over the righteous, and his ears* are open *unto their prayers: but the face of the Lord is against them that do evil. And who* is *he that will harm you, if ye be followers of that which is good? But and if ye suffer for righteousness' sake, happy* are ye: *and be not afraid of their terror, neither be troubled; But sanctify the Lord God in your hearts: and* be *ready always to* give *an answer to every man that asketh you a reason of the hope that is in you with meekness and fear: Having a good conscience; that, whereas they speak evil of you, as of evildoers, they may be ashamed that falsely accuse your good conversation [conduct] in Christ.* (1 Peter 3:12–16)

How assuring is the truth! Not only can we be confident in God's words to us; He has backed it up with evidence we carry within, "To whom God would make known what *is* the riches of the glory of this mystery among the Gentiles; which is Christ in you, the hope of glory (Colossians 1:27).

This truth reaches far beyond the self-help of positive thinking, because something has been added inside us, giving us cause to be positive. We have Christ within! It's no longer the same old you or me that we've spent a lifetime trying to retrain. It's something new that God created within each believer that empowers us to be better. Christ in you—that's the new man we get to put on. How can we miss with his spiritual nature created in us in righteousness and true holiness? The equation has changed in our favor.

Truly the comforter has come and abides within us. Everywhere believers go, the spirit of God in Christ goes with them.

◆   ◆   ◆

Truth is meant to save you first, and the comfort comes afterwards.

—Georges Bernanos

◆   ◆   ◆

CHAPTER VIII:
THE GOD OF HEALING AND RESTORATION

In the beginning, when God created the heavens and the earth, he created them in full perfection. Not one single thing was out of harmony or synchronization. Then, something disrupted the beauty and order God originally brought into existence. Understanding the cause of this upheaval will give us insight into the parentage of sickness, disease, infections, and plagues.

> In the beginning God created the heaven and the earth. And the earth was without form, and void; and darkness was upon the face of the deep. And the Spirit of God moved upon the face of the waters. (Genesis 1:1–2)

The Hebrew words translated *without form and void* can be found in Isaiah, where it clearly testifies that God had not created the world that way, but rather, it became that way:

> For thus saith the Lord that created the heavens; God himself that formed the earth and made it; he hath established it, he created it not in vain, he formed it to be inhabited: I am the Lord; and there is none else. (Isaiah 45:18)

The words *not in vain* are the same Hebrew words translated *without form and void*. If God did not create it that way, something devastating had to have occurred for this order and perfection to become corrupt and uninhabitable.

In fact, *without form* means to be laid to waste and *void* means to be put to ruin. If the earth was laid to waste and put to ruin, wouldn't those words indicate that at one time the earth had been upright and established? What induced this disastrous waste and ruin?

Biblical scholars point to Isaiah 14, Ezekiel 28, the book of Revelation, and other places to show that there was a rebellion in the spiritual sphere. Lucifer, who is now identified as Satan (among many other names), and one-third of the angelic beings tried to overthrow the kingdom of God and were ultimately cast out.

Darkness means to be deprived of light. Turning against God, who is light, these spiritual entities deprived themselves of light and became the opposite of all that light is and implies. This eclipse of evil cascaded upon them so quickly; God could not get his word in edgewise, so to speak. In this insurrection, God's magnificent creation and order became disrupted.

Ephesians indicates for whom this creation and ordered perfection was intended. It also hints at a chaotic turmoil that made it "without form and void."

> *Blessed* be *the God and Father of our Lord Jesus Christ, who hath blessed us with all spiritual blessings in heavenly* places *in Christ: According as he hath chosen us in him before the foundation of the world, that we should be holy and without blame before him in love.* (Ephesians 1:3–4)

The word *foundation* in the Greek can be translated either "to cast down" as in an overthrow or "to lie down" as in establishment.[1] If you look at it from the perspective of an overthrow, it explains what happened to the ordered universe (*kosmos*—world) in Genesis 1:2 and that our calling and choosing by God was before Lucifer's rebellion.

If we view it as an establishment, we see our calling was in the heart of God in Genesis 1:1, when all was in perfection, an ordered universe. Placing our election and choice by God in Genesis 1:1 confirms that we were not an afterthought for God; but rather, we were his first thought.

The book of Ephesians confirms that we did not corrupt the world. The epistle notes with purpose, we are to be "holy and without blame." Let the blame for the degradation of life go where it belongs, upon the princes of the darkness of this world.

The power of God cannot be restrained, nor the word of God suppressed for long. God, as corresponds with his very manner and nature, began the restoration and healing with the first recorded words of God in the Bible: "And God said, Let there be light: and there was light" (Genesis 1:3).

Immediately God set himself apart from the darkness. In this one simple command from the mouth of God, he spoke into motion the very laws of universal healing and restoration that govern all of nature and life. Our gracious God is so very loving and kind, that for the protection of all life, he designed healing into the very essence of life.

It is the basic function of life to resist and fight disease, sickness, and injury. Had God not designed life in this way, the most microscopic germ, the smallest organism, would wipe out life with impunity. There would be no way to stop the advancement of unsoundness. The first outbreak of infection would bring all life—human, animal, and vegetable—to extinction. A summer cold would be fatal. The tiniest abrasion would prove lethal, for there would be no staunching the flow of blood.

Found throughout the word of God is healing in nature through plants, herbs, minerals, and other forms. His words spoke healing and restoration into life and nature in perpetuity.

And God said, Let the earth bring forth grass, the herb yielding seed, and the fruit tree yielding fruit after his kind, whose seed is in itself, upon the earth: and it was so. And the earth brought forth grass, and

herb yielding seed after his kind, and the tree yielding fruit, whose seed
was *in itself, after his kind: and God saw that* it was *good. (Genesis*
1:11–12)

All healing begins at the word of God. Healing in itself is the redemptive nature of God manifested. God tells us:

He sent his word, and healed them, and delivered them *from their*
destructions. (Psalms 107:20)

[God] Who forgiveth all thine iniquities; who healeth all thy diseases;
Who redeemeth thy life from destruction; who crowneth thee with lov-
ing kindness and tender mercies; Who satisfieth thy mouth with good
things; so that *thy youth is renewed like the eagle's. (Psalms 103:3–5)*

All the way through the ministry of Jesus Christ we see the will of God juxtaposed against that of the devil (the thief), as shown in the following verses:

The thief cometh not, but for to steal, and to kill, and to destroy: I am
come that they might have life, and that they might have it *more*
abundantly. (John 10:10)

How God anointed Jesus of Nazareth with the Holy Ghost and with
power: who went about doing good, and healing all that were
oppressed of the devil; for God was with him. (Acts 10:38)

One may say, "I am not good enough to deserve healing;" however, God is good enough to give it. God does not heal on the basis of our goodness, but because of his own goodness and the goodness of his beloved Son, Jesus Christ. His tender mercies reach out to all mankind. Anyone who has experienced healing has been a recipient of his divine beneficence, as it says in Exodus 15:26, "for I *am* the Lord that healeth thee [thy physician]."

The title *Lord* is indicative of a pledge or covenant relationship. Healing, regeneration, and restoration are all integral to the word and will of God.

We should remember that when God created the heavens and the earth, it was perfect. When he restored it and gave the authority over it to man, it was paradise. It was when man transferred his dominion to Satan that it again fell into corruption.

Sickness, disease, disaster, and injury were unheard of in the garden. Eden flourished under the administration of Adam and Eve. Once Eve was deceived, and Adam gave over his authority, the earth once more began to degenerate and become corrupt.

In this present evil world we are surrounded by the depraved workings of Satan and his ilk. Yet by the light and laws of God, the earth is able to resist total devastation. After the ravages of floods, earthquakes, eruptions, famines, and plagues, the earth continues to regenerate and replenish. In the fullness of time, it will once again revive into a paradise and beyond.

◆　　◆　　◆

Earth hath no sorrow that heaven cannot heal.

—Sir Thomas More

◆　　◆　　◆

CHAPTER IX:
GOD IS GOOD ALWAYS

From the beginning, the God and Father of our Lord Jesus Christ has been a God of deliverance, restoration, and salvation. What a wonderful day it will be when mankind comes to the realization of God's good intent and good will toward all humanity.

> *And the angel said unto them, Fear not: for, behold, I bring you good tidings of great joy, which shall be to all people. For unto you is born this day in the city of David a Savior, which is Christ the Lord. And this shall be a sign unto you; Ye shall find the babe wrapped in swaddling clothes, lying in a manger. And suddenly there was with the angel a multitude of the heavenly host praising God, and saying, Glory to God in the highest, and on earth peace, good will toward men. (Luke 2:10–14)*

One of the hardest concepts for man to truly get his arms around is that God is good always, and that his intent toward mankind has always been good will. One elementary Scripture that should govern the hearts of mankind is the true proof of his redemptive love as so clearly expressed in John 3:16, "For God so loved the world, that he gave his only begotten Son, that whosoever believeth in him should not perish, but have everlasting life."

Let me attempt to explain some of the greatness of the depth in this verse:

For God—who is indeed the greatest

So loved—the greatest intensity

The world—the greatest number (every person)
That he gave—the greatest act
His only begotten Son—the greatest sacrifice
That whosoever—the greatest invitation
Believeth in him—the greatest simplicity
Should not perish—the greatest deliverance
But have everlasting life—the greatest gift

How vast is the heart of God! How gracious is his invitation. How simply he made this magnanimous gift available.

> *That if thou shalt confess with thy mouth the Lord Jesus, and shalt believe in thine heart that God hath raised him from the dead, thou shalt be saved. For with the heart man believeth unto righteousness; and with the mouth confession is made unto salvation. (Romans 10:9–10)*

Then comes this stunning pronouncement to all of mankind, "For God sent not his Son into the world to condemn the world; but that the world through him might be saved" (John 3:17).

Satan certainly condemns the world. Men may wish to condemn the world, but God's proclamation is that it "might be saved (restored to wholeness)." Perhaps you were taught as was I, that God would destroy the world (the planets and the inhabitants) one day. How wrongly I had been informed. How often I would lay the blame for calamities, disasters, and tragedies at the feet of God. When the truth is, salvation for humanity is available now and God will bring the earth back into perfection at the appointed time. All the time my Bible spoke clearly and definitively—*God is light and in him is no darkness at all.* As John 10:10 explains, "The thief cometh not, but for to steal, and to kill, and to destroy: I am come that they might have life, and that they might have *it* more abundantly."

It is Satan who damns the world and seeks its destruction. Christ has overcome the world. John 16:33 affirms, "These things I have spoken unto you, that in me ye might have peace. In the world ye shall have tribulation: but be of good cheer; I have overcome the world."

Until God sets in order a new heaven and a new earth wherein righteousness dwells, we will live in this present evil world. During this period we will endure the pressures of life brought on by the workings of Satan, but Jesus encourages us to *be of good cheer*, to be daring of mind. That is, take heart in our victory in Christ right now, and overcome Satan's attempts to discourage us from living joyfully.

> *For whatsoever is born of God overcometh the world: and this is the victory that overcometh the world,* even *our faith. Who is he that overcometh the world, but he that believeth that Jesus is the Son of God? (1 John 5:4–5)*

Victorious living is afresh each new day for those who believe, with glimpses of the beauty of his presence and power.

> *For now we see through a glass, darkly; but then face to face: now I know in part; but then shall I know even as also I am known. (1 Corinthians 13:12)*

Ultimately, we will have all eternity to enjoy the goodness and light of God in all its magnificence and perfection. Even the creation itself awaits these days.

> *For I reckon that the sufferings of this present time* are *not worthy* to be compared *with the glory which shall be revealed in us. For the earnest expectation of the creature [creation] waiteth for the manifestation of the sons of God. For the creature [creation] was made subject to vanity, not willingly, but by reason of him [Satan] who hath subjected* the same *in hope [while mankind awaits in hope], Because the creature [creation] itself also shall be delivered from the bondage of corruption into the glorious liberty of the children of God. For we know that the whole creation groaneth and travaileth in pain together [even] until now. (Romans 8:18–22)*

Even today, with all the evil workings of Satan, these are our days to rejoice in God's unmistakable goodness. For we know there is a future time coming when, not only for us but for the whole creation, God has planned full redemption.

> *For ye shall go out with joy, and be led forth with peace: the mountains and the hills shall break forth before you into singing, and all the trees of the field shall clap their hands. Instead of the thorn shall come up the fir tree, and instead of the brier shall come up the myrtle tree: and it shall be to the Lord for a name, for an everlasting sign that shall not be cut off. (Isaiah 55:12–13)*

When the Queen of Sheba saw the splendor of Solomon's kingdom, the wisdom of his rulership, the delight of those who served him, and "his ascent by which he went up unto the house of the Lord; there was no more spirit in her" (1 Kings 10:5). It took her breath away. When people see the presence of God and the glory of his Christ, no human words of exultation will ever utter the praises due his wisdom and ways. Were we to take all the dictionaries of all languages of all time, place them in the hands of our finest thinkers and our most gifted of poets, our efforts of expression would fall far short to describe even an instance of his gracious presence and the blessedness of his kingdom.

If you are listening closely, it is not the rustling of leaves you hear in the wind, it is the applause of a grateful creation in appreciation of your new birth and the glory to which it portends.

◆   ◆   ◆

Unhappily, I possess neither that eloquence of diction, that poetry of imagination, nor that brilliance of metaphor to tell you all that they mean.

—General Douglas MacArthur

◆   ◆   ◆

CONCLUSION: THE TRUE JUSTICE OF A JUST GOD

God, being a just and loving Father, will see that there is a true, final, and ultimate justice that will last for all time. His meted judgment will totally satisfy the hearts of those whose lives have been marred and scarred by the malfeasance and injustice perpetrated upon them by the evil spirit realm. "The Lord knoweth how to deliver the godly out of temptations, and to reserve the unjust unto the day of judgment to be punished" (2 Peter 2:9).

The temptation is, to be goaded by Satan in anger, to commit a similar act in retaliation and retribution against those persons we feel may have injured us in some way. However, God will not forget us, nor the pain and loss we have suffered. His plan gets to the very source for the execution of true justice. This plan includes our complete vindication from the workings of the satanic realm and a complete restoration of all that rightfully belonged to us.

> *Recompense to no man evil for evil. Provide things honest in the sight of all men. If it be possible, as much as lieth in you, live peaceable with all men. Dearly beloved, avenge not yourselves, but* rather *give place unto wrath: for it is written, Vengeance* is *mine; I will repay, saith the Lord. (Romans 12:17–19)*

Most people equate vengeance with a punishment of some sort. However, we just read, "Recompense to no man evil for evil." What you sow, you reap. What you give out, you get back. It is true of the negative as well as the positive. God has authored the laws of spiritual return; they are inviolate and span all time.

Mankind does not need to "settle the score." Evil will ultimately take care of itself. Let us place ourselves in the security of God's hands. Evil will break itself upon the laws of God and be its own undoing.

In Paul's epistle to Titus, Paul appointed him to ordain elders in all the churches in Crete. Paul expounded upon the qualifications or virtues these candidates should exhibit. Titus 1:7 is explicit, "For a bishop [an elder or overseer] must be blameless, as the steward of God; not selfwilled, not soon angry, not given to wine, no striker, not given to filthy lucre."

Elders are "not soon angry." There is no corresponding word for *soon* in the Greek text. The word *angry* indicates a building up of emotion to the point of seeking revenge or punishment. Elders are ones proven to exercise control over their emotions. You cannot "push their buttons." They are not ones who retaliate.

If this virtue is required of leaders, wouldn't it stand to reason that this quality is found in the heavenly Father? Especially if we are to be "followers (imitators) of God, as dear children (Ephesians 5:1).

In Romans 12:19, the word translated *vengeance* from the Greek text simply means, "the execution and maintenance of that which is right."[1] There is no indication of administering punishment or reason for pain to be inflicted by God. That would not provide man with true justice, because punishment does not return to the injured party that which is right nor restore that which was lost.

I am not speaking of the incarceration or incapacitation of criminals by judicial authorities. These may be necessary for the protection of innocence. I am speaking of the restoration of perfection God set for man in the fullness of time.

Verse 19 continues, "I will repay, saith the Lord." Not with punishment. God is not speaking to the enemies of mankind in this verse. Rather, he is addressing the believing ones! What will be repaid? God, who is good always, and exceedingly gracious, will repay to you in full for all that you have lost or had stolen, corrupted, and/or distorted.

Remember the Eastern expression "heap coals of fire on his head?" It is actually a quote taken from Proverbs 25:21–22: "If thine enemy be hungry, give him bread to eat; and if he be thirsty, give him water to drink: For thou shalt heap coals of fire upon his head, and the Lord shall reward thee."

Clearly, the one repaid is you. Your effort will be rewarded. God will repay to you what your enemies have exacted from you, and more.

> *And I will restore to you the years that the locust hath eaten, the cankerworm, and the caterpiller, and the palmerworm, my great army which I sent among you. And ye shall eat in plenty, and be satisfied, and praise the name of the Lord your God, that hath dealt wondrously with you: and my people shall never be ashamed. (Joel 2:25–26)*

There is a restoration coming, a making completely whole, and a full and total repayment. The locust, the cankerworm, the caterpillar, and the palmerworm are all euphemisms representing the evil spirit realm, how they work to strip your life. But, this just God will restore to you all the many blessings in all of their fullness.

You will *be satisfied* means that you will be totally satisfied—fullness from which there is no sense of lack. Only God can do that! No wonder Romans 12 concludes by telling us to "overcome evil with good." That's what God will do for us. All of the evil mankind has suffered and the pain and loss humanity has born will be overcome by God's goodness.

Perhaps something of yours was once lost or stolen. It may not have been worth much in dollars, but possessed sentimental value. Were it replaced with a brand new item, the personal value could not be recovered. Even if the very same object were recovered, how could you be paid sufficiently for the time it was gone?

The word translated *ashamed* means for one to be disappointed in his or her expectations. God will take care for you and in his perfect justice, will mete out to you the total restoration and complete fullness for your loss. You will not be disappointed. That is his dealing "wondrously with you." How will he do it? I do not know, but that he will do it, I am confidently assured by Romans 11:33, which says, "O the depth of the riches both of the wisdom and knowledge of God! how unsearchable *are* his judgments, and his ways past finding out!"

On the day of Jesus Christ's ascension, the apostles had an understanding of this great truth as it applied to Israel. As told in Acts 1:6, "When they therefore were come together, they asked of him, saying, Lord, wilt thou at this time restore again the kingdom to Israel?" They were not asking for the destruction and punishment of Roman occupational forces. Their interest was in the restoration of the kingdom of Israel. That is, for Israel to receive back its glory and blessing from God to be a "delightsome land."

Peter and John again referred to this restoration of Israel at the healing of the man lame from his mother's womb at the Gate called Beautiful.

> *Repent ye therefore, and be converted, that your sins may be blotted out, when the times of refreshing shall come from the presence of the Lord; And he shall send Jesus Christ, which before was preached unto you: Whom the heaven must receive until the times of restitution of all things, which God hath spoken by the mouth of all his holy prophets since the world began. (Acts 3:19–21)*

Weren't these the people who called for Jesus' crucifixion? One would think a little punishment would be in order, but their sins were going to be "blotted out." Instead, there would be a "refreshing," a recovery from toils and evil—in the presence of the Lord. Why? Because God is light and in him is no darkness at all! They would receive restitution, re-establishment, and the restoration of all the promises of God in complete fulfillment, promised since the world began.

Today is Man's Day, the day in which man does the judging. The Lord's Day is coming when he will pronounce judgments—not of condemnation, but of commendation.

> *But with me it is a very small thing that I should be judged of you, or of man's judgment: yea, I judge not mine own self. For I know nothing by myself; yet am I not hereby justified: but he that judgeth me is the Lord. Therefore judge nothing before the time, until the Lord come, who both will bring to light the hidden things of darkness, and will make manifest the counsels of the hearts: and then shall every man have praise of God. (1 Corinthians 4:3–5)*

Judgments here upon the earth, as pure hearted and as fairly as men and women are capable of judging, will never bring about true justice. Can situations be brought full circle as if the incident never happened? Consider for a moment the death penalty in a murder case. True justice would demand the murdered person be restored to life to enjoy all that was taken and to include that which had lost out on in life.

What about the one who is executed? In the olden days of England, the judge might sentence the murderer "to be hung by the neck until dead." From a legal perspective the obligation and debt to society would be fulfilled and the requirements of the law be satisfied by way of the guilty party's death. According to the law and the ruling of the judge, the commitment would terminate at the point of death. Now what? Should this person also be made alive once again? Mankind is unable to take this situation full-circle completion for either party.

Jesus Christ is God's answer to man's need for true justice. All that was lost in Adam, God recovered in Jesus Christ and much more. Thank God, there is a day coming when he will do the judging. He will truly execute and maintain that which is right and restore to man all that truly belongs to him, never to be stolen or distorted again.

At the proper time, God will execute and maintain that which is right for all time. Those who have lived during the period of the Church of

Grace, beginning from the Day of Pentecost (Acts 2) until the gathering together (1Thessalonians 4), who accepted Jesus as Lord, will "meet the Lord in the air: and so shall we ever be with [like] the Lord" (1 Thessalonians 4:17). This is Christ coming *for* his church.

Next comes the events of the book of Revelation and the prophecies of Daniel and others. This includes the ascension of the anti-Christ to the throne of the temple of God, Christ coming *with* his church, the great symbolic conflict of Armageddon, the fall of Babylon, and many other such events.

Then, the Bible talks of two resurrections: the first resurrection for the just and the second for the unjust. The resurrection of the just will consist of those who anticipated the coming of Christ throughout the Old Testament and the gospel period, who died before Pentecost, and those remaining after the Church of Grace is gathered. This will include all the men and women who have neither chosen Christ, nor were born of the seed of the serpent.

During this period when the resurrection of the just occurs, Satan will be bound for a thousand years. This will allow those from all the generations of mankind to really see the graciousness of God and have the opportunity to choose his glorious Christ without the influence and deception of Satan, his false prophets, and the rest of the evil spirit realm. Totally unencumbered, the natural man, the man of the senses, will openly see the goodness of God and the beauty of his Christ.

> *And I saw an angel come down from heaven, having the key of the bottomless pit and a great chain in his hand. And he laid hold on the dragon, that old serpent, which is the Devil, and Satan, and bound him a thousand years, And cast him into the bottomless pit, and shut him up, and set a seal upon him, that he should deceive the nations no more, till the thousand years should be fulfilled: and after that he must be loosed a little season. (Revelation 20:1–3)*

When men and women peer into the unobstructed view of what Jesus, who is the Christ, truly gained for them by the sacrifice of himself; mankind will drop to its knees in honor of that most noble name. He is the savior for the whole world!

> *Wherefore God also hath highly exalted him, and given him a name which is above every name: That at the name of Jesus every knee should bow, of things in heaven, and things in earth, and things under the earth; And that every tongue should confess that Jesus Christ is Lord, to the glory of God the Father. (Philippians 2:9–11)*

> *Therefore judge nothing before the time, until the Lord come, who both will bring to light the hidden things of darkness, and will make manifest the counsels of the hearts: and then shall every man have praise of God. (1 Corinthians 4:5)*

Is this an indictment against mankind? Do we have to dread having all the hidden things, our faults and failings, our secret sins, revealed before all? Will all of our private thoughts be played upon the big screen for all to see? No, the "hidden things of darkness" and "the counsels of the hearts" are not in reference to our secret sins that we never told anyone about or no one ever knew. God is love and good always. There is no need or purpose for any man or woman to be put to open shame. Rather, the Scripture says "then shall every man have praise of God."

At that time, when the glorified Christ comes, what will be exposed for all to see are the secret workings of Satan, the functioning of the evil spirit realm to dissuade the hearts of men and women from Christ and how they kept men and women from choosing Christ at the first opportunity to believe. Yet thankfully, in all their persuasion, coercion, and pressure, these deceivers could not convince these pure-hearted people to choose the evil one as their god. They shall receive the praise or commendation of God.

As a significant portion of this revealing of Christ and the glory of our God, the believing ones of today will serve and be honored in a uniquely wonderful way. The book of Ephesians gives a glimpse into the reward for our trust in the word of truth, the good news of our salvation, and the hope of our calling.

> *That in the ages to come he might shew the exceeding riches of his grace in* his *kindness toward us through Christ Jesus. For we are his workmanship, created in Christ Jesus unto good works, which God hath before ordained that we should walk in them. (Ephesians 2:7, 10)*

The word *shew* means to put on display. *For we are his workmanship* is "a thing produced, as with effort, object and design."[2] If what is on display was created in Christ Jesus and was done by God with effort, it must be his *magnum opus, pièce de résistance*; a masterwork of perfection! The believing ones will be the showcase of God's magnificent handiwork in Christ to exhibit his grace and kindness.

While in this life, as we walk according to the Scriptures, we depict the majestic brilliance of God to the world. For those who have hunger of the heart and eyes to see, flashes the awesome craftsmanship of the Creator, loosely veiled by our flesh. Then (*voilà*), comes the full display of the *Believing One's Hall of Fame.*

We will not be standing on a pedestal in a gallery, but we will be the living, moving representation of the "good works, which God hath before ordained that we should walk." Every act of love for God and every heart won for Christ will be personified. We have played and will play a grand part in the reason every knee shall bow and every tongue (all of the people and in all of the languages) shall confess Jesus Christ is Lord, to the glory of God the Father.

Then the twelve apostles will sit upon thrones to give righteous judgment to the believing ones and to honor the faithful.

And I saw thrones, and they sat upon them, and judgment was given unto them: and I saw the souls of them that were beheaded for the witness of Jesus, and for the word of God, and which had not worshipped the beast, neither his image, neither had received his mark upon their foreheads, or in their hands; and they lived and reigned with Christ a thousand years. But the rest of the dead lived not again until the thousand years were finished. This is the first resurrection. (Revelation 20:4–5)

The number "one thousand" represents the complete cycle of judgment. There were ten plagues upon the Egyptians, leading to the release and deliverance of the children of Israel. A thousand is ten to the third power, making the cycle for judgment absolutely complete. Those in the resurrection of the just have received the full and final judgment to eternal life, to live unobstructed in the presence of God and his glorious Christ.

The second resurrection is for the unjust. It is for those who are born of the seed of the serpent. These are people who have been hopelessly deceived to believe that the devil is the true God. These are the ones who have "his mark upon their foreheads," signifying their minds are forever unchangeable. And *in their hands* symbolizes their dedicated action in service to Satan. They have rejected Jesus Christ, the savior from sin, and the saving grace of God. This is the unforgivable sin.

Genesis sets the two spiritual sources for seed: the seed of the serpent and the seed of the woman, being Christ. Genesis 3:14a and 15 says: "And the Lord God said unto the serpent, And I will put enmity [a state of hostility] between thee and the woman, and between thy seed and her seed; it shall bruise thy head, and thou shalt bruise his heel."

In a confrontation with the Pharisees, Jesus addresses the two sources of seed and the two fathers.

I speak that which I have seen with my Father: and ye do that which ye have seen with your father. Jesus said unto them, If God were your Father, ye would love me: for I proceeded forth and came from God;

neither came I of myself, but he sent me. Ye are of your Father the devil, and the lusts of your father ye will do. He was a murderer from the beginning, and abode not in the truth, because there is no truth in him. When he speaketh a lie, he speaketh of his own: for he is a liar, and the father of it. (John 8:38, 42, 44)

Men and women who are born of the seed of the serpent will see the second death following this great white throne judgment of the unjust.

And I saw the dead, small and great, stand before God; and the books were opened: and another book was opened, which is the book of life: and the dead were judged out of those things which were written in the books, according to their works. And the sea gave up the dead which were in it; and death and hell delivered up the dead which were in them: and they were judged every man according to their works. And death and hell [the grave] were cast into the lake of fire. This is the second death. And whosoever was not found written in the book of life was cast into the lake of fire. (Revelation 20:12–15)

However, prior to seeing the second death, they will be alive again when Satan is "loosed for a season." That is when the restraints are taken off him and the people who chose him to be their true god get to feel the full weight of his "fellowship."

The second death implies that they will cease to exist. Jude, verses 12 and 13, affirm they are "trees whose fruit withereth, without fruit, twice dead … to whom is reserved the blackness of darkness for ever." *Twice* indicates something is established and unchanging. *Twice dead* would imply no life ever again. The same sense is conveyed by *the blackness of darkness for ever*. They will never, ever exist again!

However, it is not the true God that brings even the second death. Death is an enemy and in the power of the devil. Remember, 1 Corinthians 15:26: "The last enemy *that* shall be destroyed *is* death." And Hebrews 2:14: "Forasmuch then as the children are partakers of flesh and blood, he [Jesus] also himself likewise took part of the same; that through death he might destroy him that had the power of death, that is, the devil."

The devil has the power of death, both the first and second death. Our God is the author of life. He has the power to make alive from the dead, as demonstrated in the resurrections. He just will not exercise that option over the second death. He will not extend his grace and mercy at that point (Exodus 33:19).

God will not need to destroy the evil spirit realm. Evil is restrained by light. Without restraint, evil will self destruct.

> *And the devil that deceived them was cast into the lake of fire and brimstone, where the beast and the false prophet are, and shall be tormented day and night for ever and ever. (Revelation 20:10)*

Fire requires fuel to burn. The absolute hate and darkness of the devil and his unholy angels provide the fuel. The word *tormented* is used of a touchstone and means to rub against. The indication here is that the devil and all the evil spirits that have troubled us will provide their own fuel as they rub their iniquitous nature against each other.

There is coming a new heaven and earth wherein dwells righteousness. In this new heaven and earth, we will never again be separated from fellowship with God.

> *And I heard a great voice out of heaven saying, Behold, the tabernacle of God is with men, and he will dwell with them, and they shall be his people, and God himself shall be with them, and be their God. And God shall wipe away all tears from their eyes; and there shall be no more death, neither sorrow, nor crying, neither shall there be any more pain: for the former things are passed away. And he that sat upon the throne said, Behold, I make all things new. And he said unto me, Write: for these words are true and faithful. (Revelation 21:3–5)*

God's flawless plan for redemption and justice shall be entirely complete. This is the anticipated hope we have that gives us patience in these days when man does the judging. For we know that the day is coming when God's judgment will fully satisfy the longing hearts of mankind. We should renounce thinking of God as a stern ruler and wrathful judge. He is a loving Father and the God of light. Our lives can experience fullness of joy, walking in the light, in full-sharing fellowship with him.

EPILOGUE:
LET US BE CONSTRAINED
BY LOVE

When I was a child, fear of my parents' punishment never restrained me from acting improperly. It was the benefits from enjoying their loving presence and the sweetness of our fellowship together that promoted my obedience. Within their loving care and attention, I was cherished, and all my needs were met. At the close of summer, my parents always took me shopping for school clothes, books, and a winter coat. Without ever asking, they completely provided for me with the best they could afford. How much more will our heavenly Father provide?

But my God shall supply all your need according to his riches in glory by Christ Jesus. (Philippians 4:19)

Therefore I say unto you, Take no thought [to have anxiety that distracts and divides the mind[1]] for your life, what ye shall eat, or what ye shall drink; nor yet for your body, what ye shall put on. Is not the life more than meat, and the body than raiment? Behold the fowls of the air: for they sow not, neither do they reap, nor gather into barns; yet your heavenly Father feedeth them. Are ye not much better than they? Which of you by taking thought can add one cubit unto his stature? And why take ye thought for raiment? Consider the lilies of the field, how they grow; they toil not, neither do they spin: And yet I say unto you, That even Solomon in all his glory was not arrayed like one of these. Wherefore, if God so clothe the grass of the field, which to day is, and to morrow is cast into the oven, shall he not much more clothe you, O ye of little faith? Therefore take no thought, saying, What shall

we eat? or, What shall we drink? or Wherewithal shall we be clothed?
(For after all these things do the Gentiles seek:) for your heavenly
Father knoweth that ye have need of all these things. But seek ye first
the kingdom of God, and his righteousness; and all these things shall
be added unto you. (Matthew 6:25–33)

If God can be so gracious to us in this life and so much the more throughout eternity, how could our hearts not be constrained by his loving care? Seeking the kingdom of God entails endeavoring to walk in love and walk in light, even as he is light. To bring as much joy, and love, and peace, and deliverance as we can into this present world that we may shine the light of Christ unto those who sit in darkness.

The world has seen enough harshness, hardness of heart, criticism, skepticism, sarcasm, and cynicism. It may be easy to get caught up in all the reasoning to hate, dislike, and despise, but consider these verses:

For it is impossible for those who were once enlightened, and have
tasted of the heavenly gift, and were made partakers of the Holy Ghost
[to partake of the new birth], And have tasted the good word of God,
and the powers of the world to come, If they shall fall away, to renew
them again unto repentance; seeing they crucify to themselves the Son
of God afresh, and put him *to an open shame. (Hebrews 6:4–6)*

The love Christ has for us is a love that endures; it is unlimited in compassion and immeasurable in mercy. It elevates the heart in hope and gives us courage to stand. His love constrains us. If we "have tasted the good word of God and the powers of the world to come," if we have known "the love of Christ, which passeth knowledge" (Ephesians 3:19), then our hearts would forbid us from bringing dishonor to his notable name. Doing so would be like an anchor or a millstone hung around the neck—a weight far too much to bear.

"Seeing they crucify to themselves the Son of God afresh, and put *him* to an open shame" does not refer to the loss of eternal life, but to the tremendous burden it would be to walk in this life, as one who is so beloved. Love, not fear, motivates the heart of a believing one.

In the Eastern cultures, a man's name was to be greatly revered. A person in trouble could receive mercy by calling upon the name of a great one. If that person acted dishonorably, though calling upon that worthy name, his plea for mercy might not be taken seriously; in fact, his actions would bring mockery to the name of that great one.

So we present ourselves worthy of that name when we call upon the name of Christ Jesus. We identify with the name of Christ and we redirect our lives to magnify his name. The love of Christ constrains us. We allow our lives to tell the story unimpaired.

> *Only let your conversation [manner in which you conduct your life] be as it becometh the gospel of Christ: that whether I come and see you, or else be absent, I may hear of your affairs, that ye stand fast in one spirit, with one mind striving together for the faith of the gospel. (Philippians 1:27)*

> *Wherefore, my beloved, as ye have always obeyed, not as in my presence only, but now much more in my absence, work out your own salvation [wholeness] with fear and trembling [awe and respect for that name by which God purchased your salvation]. (Philippians 2:12)*

This constraining love begins first in the family of God.

> *A new commandment I give unto you, That ye love one another; as I have loved you, that ye also love one another. By this shall all men know that ye are my disciples, if ye have love one to another. (John 13:34–35)*

Why would love of one another be a sign of discipleship? Matthew 22:35–40 explains:

> *Then one of them, which was a lawyer, asked him a question, tempting him, and saying, Master, which is the great commandment in the*

law? Jesus said unto him, Thou shalt love the Lord thy God with all thy heart, and with all thy soul, and with all thy mind. This is the first and great commandment. And the second is like unto it, Thou shalt love thy neighbor as thyself. On these two commandments hang all the law and the prophets.

The words *like unto* mean resemble, equally united, or to give an external form or appearance of what one has internally. The word *it* refers back to the first and great commandment. One cannot give an external showing of his or her love for God without loving their neighbor as themself. To love God with all your heart, soul, and mind is demonstrated in your love to your neighbor. You cannot do one without the other. They are equally united. To break the bond by which they are joined is to break the commandment.

The word *hang* means to be suspended, that is, to be supported from above. When you and I walk in love the law is suspended. It remains at rest because it is not needed. The law is for those who do not love or do not wish to live this love from God. As Paul wrote to Timothy, "Knowing this, that the law is not made for the righteous man, but for the lawless" (1 Timothy 1:9). The law will have consequences. As we have seen, it can condemn but it cannot convert, convict but not redeem, and punish but it cannot heal. In living outside of the love of God we find only the law and its consequences. The saying—"No one is above the law" is true if it is not the law of the love of God in Christ Jesus. Under its grand arch suspends all the rest of the laws.

The "first and great commandment" is to love God. *First* is "foremost; in place, order, time, or dignity." *Great* means vast in magnitude and value. While the second is indeed, like unto it.

If a man say, I love God, and hateth his brother, he is a liar: for he that loveth not his brother whom he hath seen, how can he love God whom he hath not seen? And this commandment have we from him, That he who loveth God loveth his brother also. (1 John 4:20–21)

The Greek word translated *hateth* is deeply revealing as it was used among the classic writers. It held the idea of being hated by the gods. As one author wrote, "I believed he was in love with me, but he hates me as though it were a divine command."[2]

When a believing one demonstrates hatred toward a brother in Christ, it communicates as if that brother were hated by God. It is even more serious if that believing one is an elder or minister in the church. To that brother in Christ, the elder or minister represents the will of God. Yet, he represents to this young one that he is no longer loved by the Father of light. How devastating that must be to the heart of a young believer. While it makes the minister a liar against the truth because the Scripture tells us that nothing "shall be able to separate us from the love of God, which is in Christ Jesus our Lord" (Romans 8:39).

The King James Version of the Holy Bible states, "On these two commandments hang all the law and the prophets." The Amplified Bible reads, "These two commandments sum up *and* upon them depend all the Law and the Prophets." If you have broken either part, you have broken the whole of all of the law and all of the prophecy.

The courts warn us, the elders implore us, the daysman beseech us, the comforter exhorts us, and the love of our Christ constrains us:

Be ye therefore followers of God, as dear children; And walk in love, as Christ also hath loved us, and hath given himself for us an offering and a sacrifice to God for a sweetsmelling savour. (Ephesians 5:1–2)

Yet this constraining love does not stop there. God's love is so powerful and the love of Christ is so compelling; we are given the charge to love even our enemies.

But love ye your enemies, and do good, and lend, hoping for nothing again; and your reward shall be great, and ye shall be the children of the Highest: for he is kind unto the unthankful and to the evil. (Luke 6:35)

How do we love our enemies? We love our enemies the same way in which God loved us when we were enemies to God and the things of God. He reconciled us! Colossians 1:21 says, "And you, that were sometime alienated and enemies in *your* mind by wicked works, yet now hath he reconciled." Remember, the real enemy of humanity is the evil spirit realm exerting their influence upon the minds of mankind. In contrast, we extend the love and goodness of God.

The natural man's innate drive is to achieve justice through punishment. The spiritual man understands that true justice is in the power and goodness of God where injury can give way to healing and condemnation to conversion.

> *And all things* are *of God, who hath reconciled us to himself by Jesus Christ, and hath given to us the ministry [service] of reconciliation; To wit, that God was in Christ, reconciling the world unto himself, not imputing their trespasses unto them; and hath committed unto us the word of reconciliation. Now then we are ambassadors [elders] for Christ, as though God did beseech* you *by us: we pray* you *in Christ's stead, be ye reconciled to God. (2 Corinthians 5:18–20)*

An elder for Christ, with the proper heart and purpose of the Scriptures, has the ideal solutions; not from traditions or religious ritual, but by "the word of reconciliation," full of mercies and compassions for the weaknesses of mankind.

Neither elected nor appointed by men, born-again ones, in Christ's stead, can reconcile men and women back to God. Walking in the light allows us to serve in the magnanimous position of a daysman for the believing ones of today.

Through the years we may have affection for many people—but the measure of our lives will be what we have done by our love for one man—Jesus Christ of Nazareth, the only begotten Son of God and the savior for the whole world.

What is our future? Eternity with God who is light and in him is no darkness at all. Therein is the true justice of a just God.

◆   ◆   ◆

May all of our thoughts, words, and deeds abundantly serve our Lord Jesus Christ.

—Lawrence A. Panarello

◆   ◆   ◆

THE BELIEVING ONE'S
HALL OF FAME

We often refer to Hebrews 11, as the "Believing One's Hall of Fame."
And somewhere in those hallowed halls is a place set for your name.
For just one of the days you've lived, no treasure could afford,
Nor ready scribe with pen in hand could diligently record
All the mighty works you do, from beginning to the last;
Every promise from the Word of God you've believed and brought to pass;
Every act in kindness done, with love, throughout your life;
Every single soul you've won, and led their hearts to Christ.
No, not one line, nor act, nor deed is forgotten to depart.
The Father, for His child, keeps a living record in his heart.
He'll place a plaque of purest gold, inscribed with greatest care,
"To my child, in whom I'm well pleased—a believer extraordinaire."
And so throughout all eternity, on display for all to view,
In the Hall of Fame—God's own heart—is that place set just for you.

—Lawrence A. Panarello

END NOTES

Introduction

[1] Kittel, Gerhardt (ed.), *Theological Dictionary of the New Testament, (Vol. I-X)*, Grand Rapids, MI: Eerdmans, reprinted 1933, Vol. II, 577.

[2] Bullinger, E. W., *Figures of Speech Used in The Bible*, Grand Rapids, MI: Baker Book House, reprinted 1968, 871.

[3] Bullinger, E. W., *Figures of Speech Used in The Bible*, Grand Rapids, MI: Baker Book House, reprinted 1968, 405.

[4] Bullinger, E. W., *Figures of Speech Used in The Bible*, Grand Rapids, MI: Baker Book House, reprinted 1968, 823.

[5] Houghton Mifflin, *Second College Edition: The American Heritage Dictionary*, Boston, MA: Houghton Mifflin, 1991, 639.

[6] Kittel, Gerhardt (ed.), *Theological Dictionary of the New Testament, (Vol. I-X)*, Grand Rapids, MI: Eerdmans, reprinted 1933, Vol. II, 908.

Chapter One: The True Justice of a Just God

[1] Pillai, Bishop K. C., Light Through an Eastern Window, *Laws and Justice*, New Knoxville, OH: American Christian, reprinted 1985, 71–87.

Chapter Two: The Civil Court or Tribunal

[1] Knight, K. C., *The Catholic Encyclopedia, Sanhedrin, Vol. XIII, Online Edition*, 2003, http://www.newadvent.org/cathen/13444a.htm.

[2] Pillai, Bishop K. C., Light Through an Eastern Window, *Laws and Justice*, New Knoxville, OH: American Christian, reprinted 1985, 71–87.

[3] Pillai, Bishop K. C., Light Through an Eastern Window, *Laws and Justice*, New Knoxville, OH: American Christian, reprinted 1985, 112–113.

[4] Bullinger, E. W., *Figures of Speech Used in The Bible,* Grand Rapids, MI: Baker Book House, reprinted 1968, 823.

Chapter Three: The Elders of the Gate

[1] Pillai, Bishop K. C., Light Through an Eastern Window, *Laws and Justice,* New Knoxville, OH: American Christian, reprinted 1985, 71–87.
[2] Pillai, Bishop K. C., Light Through an Eastern Window, *Laws and Justice,* New Knoxville, OH: American Christian, reprinted 1985, 71–87.
[3] Bullinger, E. W., *A Critical Lexicon and Concordance to the English and Greek New Testament,* Grand Rapids, MI: Kregel, published 1999, 317.

Chapter Four: The Daysman

[1] Pillai, Bishop K. C., Light Through an Eastern Window, *Laws and Justice,* New Knoxville, OH: American Christian, reprinted 1985, 71–87.

Chapter Five: The Promised Daysman

[1] Bullinger, E. W., *A Critical Lexicon and Concordance to the English and Greek New Testament,* Grand Rapids, MI: Kregel, published 1999, 492.
[2] Bullinger, E. W., *A Critical Lexicon and Concordance to the English and Greek New Testament,* Grand Rapids, MI: Kregel, published 1999, 827.
[3] Bullinger, E. W., *A Critical Lexicon and Concordance to the English and Greek New Testament,* Grand Rapids, MI: Kregel, published 1999, 834.

Chapter Six: The Pivotal Day for Mankind

[1] Bullinger, E. W., *A Critical Lexicon and Concordance to the English and Greek New Testament,* Grand Rapids, MI: Kregel, published 1999, 577.

Chapter Seven: The Comforter Comes

[1] Bullinger, E. W., *A Critical Lexicon and Concordance to the English and Greek New Testament,* Grand Rapids, MI: Kregel, published 1999, 168.

[2] Bullinger, E. W., *A Critical Lexicon and Concordance to the English and Greek New Testament,* Grand Rapids, MI: Kregel, published 1999, 305.

Chapter Eight: The God of Healing and Restoration

[1] Bullinger, E. W., *A Critical Lexicon and Concordance to the English and Greek New Testament,* Grand Rapids, MI: Kregel, published 1999, 305.

Conclusion: The True Justice of a Just God

[1] Bullinger, E. W., *A Critical Lexicon and Concordance to the English and Greek New Testament,* Grand Rapids, MI: Kregel, published 1999, 845.

[1] Bullinger, E. W., *A Critical Lexicon and Concordance to the English and Greek New Testament,* Grand Rapids, MI: Kregel, published 1999, 901.

Epilogue: Let Us Be Constrained by Love

[1] Bullinger, E. W., *A Critical Lexicon and Concordance to the English and Greek New Testament,* Grand Rapids, MI: Kregel, published 1999, 796.

[2] Kittel, Gerhardt (ed.), *Theological Dictionary of the New Testament,* (Vol. 1-X), Grand Rapids, MI: Eerdmans, reprinted 1933, Vol. IV, 683, Footnote [1]

If this book has been a help to you or if you would like to know more about our work with Beloved of God Ministries, please email us at:

minister@bgm-usa.org

or write to us at:

Beloved of God Ministries, Inc.

Beloved of God Ministries, Inc.
P.O. Box 594
Maynard, MA 01754   USA '94

We would love to hear from you.

www. my internet chapel. org

978-0-595-41546-5
0-595-41546-6

Breinigsville, PA USA
01 February 2010
231668BV00006B/2/A